DEMONS
IN THE WORLD
TODAY

DEMONS
IN THE WORLD
TODAY

A Study of Occultism
in the Light of God's Word

Merrill F. Unger, Th.D., Ph.D.

TYNDALE HOUSE PUBLISHERS
Wheaton, Illinois

Coverdale House Publishers Ltd. London, England

Library of Congress Catalog Card Number 72-123285
ISBN 8423-0660-9 cloth; 8423-0661-7 paper.

Eighth printing, August 1974
125,000 copies in print

Printed in the United States of America.

Contents

CHAPTER 1

Demons and the Supernatural

This is an age of phenomenal progress in man's conquest of the universe. Awestruck observers are flocking to the altars erected by science to revere human achievements in the realm of natural law. Meanwhile, the altars of God are forsaken as naturalism in theology threatens to eliminate the supernatural from everyday thought and life.

The situation is particularly ironical to the Christian who sees God permitting man to achieve feats bordering on the miraculous. Why should man become skeptical and apathetic toward religious supernaturalism at a time when science is demonstrating how "close" the natural and the supernatural can be?

The fact that supernaturalism embraces not only the morally good — God and his elect angels — but the morally evil — Satan and the fallen angels or demons — aggravates modern man's unbelief. For while some men have always denied the existence of God and the holy angels, skepticism has especially attended the sphere of evil supernaturalism. Many who profess faith in God question the existence of a personal devil and casually relegate evil spirits or demons to the realm of folklore and superstition.

Do demons exist?

If Satan and demons are merely the creation of superstition and imagination, the whole field of demonism belongs to the world of fairy tale and folklore, and not to the sphere of Chris-

7

tian theology. If there are no demons, evil cannot be traced to their activity and depraved aspects of human behavior must be attributed to other causes.

Biblical evidence

The Word of God attests the reality of evil supernaturalism through the career of both Satan and his myriads of helpers called demons or evil spirits (Luke 10:17, 20). Satan is presented as Lucifer, the first and most glorious creature of God, who subsequently sinned (Isaiah 14:12, 13; Ezekiel 28:11-19; Revelation 12:7-10). In his rebellion, Lucifer drew a multitude of angels with him and became "Satan," a Hebrew word meaning "opposer" or "adversary."

Satan reigns over a kingdom of darkness organized in opposition to God (Matthew 12:26). This opposition crystallizes in connection with man and God's purpose for him upon the earth (Genesis 3:1-15). The angels who followed Satan became the demons or evil spirits, Satan's minions.

Scripture not only presents a full-orbed picture of Satan's past, present, and future, it reveals the role of demons as Satan's powerful helpers in his opposition to God and man.

Scripture explains the reason why satanic and demonic malevolence is directed so relentlessly against man and the earth. Apparently Lucifer, the first of the angels, was created to have dominion over the earth (Job 38:1-7; Ezekiel 28:11-19). Satan was exalted and sinless before he rebelled and brought judgment and chaos upon the earth.

The Creator was now faced with the problem of evil and sin in a hitherto sinless universe. God chose the earth as the theater in which to present the great drama of human redemption. This great redemptive demonstration not only shows how God, in his infinite love and holiness, deals with evil, it will culminate in the conquest of sin, its banishment from a sin-scarred universe, and its rigid isolation for all eternity, together with its perpetrators, in a place of confinement called "the lake of fire," Gehenna or eternal hell (Revelation 20:11-15).

Until that conquest, Scripture reveals, an intense struggle rages between "the seed of the serpent," Satan with his demon hordes, and "the seed of the woman," the virgin-born Redeemer (Genesis 3:15). The Old Testament is replete with demonological phenomena because since the Fall of man in the Garden of Eden, God's saints have been the object of satanic attack (cf. Genesis 4:1-6; 6:1-10). Israel was surrounded by pagan nations which manifested the whole gamut of demonological practices and beliefs and clashed with Israel's monotheistic faith. Enlightened Israelites regarded idols as demons worshiped by man (Baruch 4:7; Psalm 95:5 Septuagint, 1 Corinthians 10:20); and the *shedhim* (Deuteronomy 32:17; Psalm 106:36, 37) and *seirim* (Leviticus 17:7; 2 Chronicles 11:15; Isaiah 13:21; 34:14) were demonic conceptions.

The New Testament presents overwhelming evidence for the existence of demons. Jesus' powerful spiritual ministry precipitated a violent outburst of evil supernaturalism. Satan and demons opposed his mighty mission among men, knowing well it would lead to their own undoing (Matthew 4:1-10; Mark 5:1-10). Our Lord gave his disciples authority to expel demons (Matthew 10:1) and expelled them himself (Matthew 15:22, 28), viewing his conquest over the demons as over Satan (Luke 10:17, 18).

The New Testament speaks of demons (James 2:19; Revelation 9:20), describes their nature (Luke 4:33; 6:18), their activity (1 Timothy 4:1; Revelation 16:14), their opposition to the believer (Ephesians 6:10-20), their abode (Luke 8:31; Revelation 9:11) and their eternal doom (Matthew 25:41).

Physical evidence

The tormentors and troublemakers of nature offer an interesting analogy to the evil agencies of the spiritual realm. In the plant kingdom, pests, insects, and blight continually harass the farmer. In the animal kingdom, all creatures have their deadly enemy. And the human body is relentlessly attacked by a multitude of bacteria which cause disease and death.

Those who hesitate to accept the testimony of Scripture about the reality of demons may thus find both scientific and philosophical corroboration in nature which has been called God's "oldest testament." The natural world vividly illustrates the activity of demonic beings in the spiritual world.

Historical evidence

The history of various religions from the earliest times shows belief in Satan and demons to be universal. According to the Bible, degeneration from monotheism resulted in the blinding of men by Satan and the most degrading forms of idolatry (Romans 1:21-32; 2 Corinthians 4:4). By the time of Abraham (c. 2000 B.C.), men had sunk into a crass polytheism that swarmed with evil spirits. Spells, incantations, magical texts, exorcisms, and various forms of demonological phenomena abound in archaeological discoveries from Sumeria and Babylon. Egyptian, Assyrian, Chaldean, Greek, and Roman antiquity are rich in demonic phenomena. The deities worshiped were invisible demons represented by material idols and images.[1]

The great ethnic faiths of India, China, and Japan major in demonism, as well as the animistic religions of Africa, South America, and some islands. Even the ancient Bible lands swarmed with demons. As George W. Gilmore declares: "The entire religious provenience out of which Hebrew religion sprang is full of demonism."[2] Early Christianity rescued its converts from the shackles of Satan and demons (Ephesians 2:2; Colossians 1:13). To an amazing degree, the history of religion is an account of demon-controlled religion, particularly in its clash with the Hebrew faith and later with Christianity.[3]

Existential evidence

The crimes, atrocities, and immoralities of ancient and modern society point to the existence of vile spirits that take possession of men's minds and bodies and drive them to wickedness and depravity (Romans 1:24-32; Ephesians 2:2-4; Revelation 9:20, 21). Because of human nature itself, "The belief in evil spirits is universal," as Davies observes.[4] Because men sense the power of Satan and demons in their lives, their belief in evil supernaturalism has been as "persistent and widespread . . . as belief in God, in good angels, or in the soul's immortality."[5]

Some men believe in Satan and demons because they *know* the power of Satan and demons in their lives, just as those who believe in Christ *know* God and the power of the Holy Spirit. Such belief is not only the result of experience but also of instinct. God, as Creator of the human mind with its instinctive propensities, has given us a primitive revelation of both good and evil supernaturalism. The basic truths of this revelation have been perpetuated by a God-given instinct attested in human experience and verifiable by observation of psychic phenomena in the realm of the occult.

The actions of the drunkard, the criminal, the libertine, the psychically and emotionally disturbed, the dope addict, the gambler, and the suicidal person (cf. John 8:44; Luke 22:3) are often caused by influences beyond mental or physical injury or disease. The strongest evidence outside the Bible that wicked and unclean spiritual agencies can enslave their victims and drive them to self-destruction is provided by people who deliberately plunge into evil, fully aware of the disastrous consequences.

People who dabble in the occult and in magical arts are recklessly flirting with demonism. Ancient pagan practices find their counterpart in today's spiritistic activities and psychical research.

Moses warned Israel of the dangers of occultism as the nation prepared to enter Canaan, where demon-energized practices flourished. "When you reach the land which the Lord your God is giving you, do not learn to imitate the obnoxious ways of those nations. There must not be found among you anyone who makes his son or daughter pass through the fire, anyone practicing divination or soothsaying, observing omens, applying sorcery, a charmer, a medium, a wizard, or a necromancer. For all who do these things are offensive to the Lord, and because of these abominable practices the Lord your God will be driving out these nations from before you" (Deuteronomy 19:9-13, Berkeley).

Human sacrifice to appease an angry deity (demon) was a particularly loathsome practice of Israel's neighbors, the Ammonites. They presented their children as a fire offering to the god Molech, a cruel form of worship that displays all the marks of Satan (John 8:44; cf. 1 Kings 11:7; 2 Kings 21:6; 23:10). This murderous practice was rigidly banned from Israel (Leviticus 18:21; 20:1-5).

Divination or soothsaying is the art of obtaining unlawful knowledge of the future. The methods violate God's holiness. In inspirational divination, the medium is under the direct influence or control of evil spirits or demons. The same is true of the modern spiritistic séance. The spiritistic agent claims to obtain the occult information from the deceased and is called a "medium" (i.e., in Hebrew, "one making inquiry of a divining demon") or "necromancer" (in Hebrew, "one seeking among the dead").

Augury, in contrast to divination, is based on the agent's or augur's interpretation of certain signs or omens in the sky, in the livers of animals, etc. This type of primitive occultism has its modern analogies in fortune-telling astrology, palmistry, cartomancy, the divining rod or pendulum, a mirror or crystal ball (mirror-mantic), and in forms of clairvoyance (called psychometry) in which objects are examined to give information about the owner.

Sorcery is a more general term to designate the practice of magic through occult formulas, incantations, and mystic mutterings. It goes beyond augury and includes the whole field of divinatory occultism. A charmer is a sorcerer who performs supernatural feats. A wizard (in Hebrew, "one who knows") is a male medium who receives superhuman knowledge through his contacts with demons. The female medium who possesses such knowledge is called a witch in the Authorized Version, better translated sorceress by the Revisers of 1884.

To the question, "Do demons actually exist?" the answer is an emphatic "yes."[6] Evidence from Scripture, nature, history of comparative religions, and human experience all testify to the existence of evil supernaturalism. In this realm, the invisible, hierarchical, spiritual personalities operate who are called "principalities . . . powers . . . world rulers of this darkness . . . spirits of wickedness in the heavenly realms" (Ephesians 6:12, Greek). These spiritual agencies are servants of Satan, "the prince of the power of the air, the spirit that now worketh in the children of disobedience" (Ephesians 2:2).

According to Scripture, Satan and demons not only exist, but they work among humanity, particularly in those who, like Satan, disdain God and openly rebel against his laws. Demonism certainly impinges on human experience and human conduct (Ephesians 2:2). Pastoral counseling, psychiatric and psychological therapy, and even medical treatment should take these demonic factors into consideration.

Who are the demons?

The precise identity of demons cannot be determined, because the Bible is silent on the issue. Because Scripture does not reveal exactly who the demons are or how they came into being, numerous theories have been advanced to account for their origin.

Incorrect theories

Demon possession is not merely a superstitious explanation of certain diseases. Such rationalizing does not define the phenomenon of evil spirits but merely explains them away. To say that demon possession in the time of Christ or in nineteenth-century China was nothing more than the effect of "certain diseases superstitiously regarded as due to demonical influence," as Davies[7] does, clashes with all the evidence of Scripture, history, and human experience.

Demons are the not the spirits of deceased men. Josephus, the Jewish historian, was apparently persuaded of this idea when he viewed demons as: "the spirits of the wicked that enter into men that are alive."[8] This explanation is apparently a reflection of Greek thought and has no foundation in biblical truth.

Demons are not the disembodied spirits of a pre-Adamite race of humanity on the earth. The whole idea of a pre-Adamite "human" race or "men in the flesh"[9] is pure conjecture. The only created beings revealed to have existed before the creation of man are angels. Moreover, the rigid distinction between "angel" and "spirit," which this theory demands, is questionable since Scripture refers to angels as spirits (Psalm 104:4; Hebrews 1:14) and sometimes uses the term "angel" for the spirit of man (Matthew 18:10; Acts 12:15).

The classical Greek meaning of the term "demons," denoting "the good spirits of departed men of the golden age" as in Hesiod,[10] is at complete variance with the uniform New Testament usage of the word. The word "demon," like other distinctive biblical words in Greek, was divinely molded through the pre-Christian centuries for its unique New Testament usage. To use its originally pagan concepts as the basis of a theory is totally unwarranted.

Demons are not the unnatural offspring of angels and antediluvian women. Two premises are necessary to establish this theory. The first is that "the sons of God" of Genesis 6:2 are fallen angels who had intercourse with mortal women, producing a mongrel race, partly human and partly angelic, called *nephilim* in Hebrew (fallen ones), rendered "giants." This term refers not so much to human size and strength, but to the Greek *gegenes* (earth born), and is used for the mythical Titans, who were partly of celestial and partly of terrestrial origin. That these "sons of God" were angels and not "godly Sethites," as some scholars maintain,[11] is supported by the uniform use of that term in the Old Testament, where it appears restricted to angelic beings (Job 1:6; 2:1; 38:7).

Although the first premise of the above theory seems established, the second is mere supposition in the face of the silence of revelation. It is pure speculation to imagine that the monstrous offspring of fallen angels and corrupt pre-flood women became disembodied spirits or demons after their bodies were destroyed in the deluge. That the fallen angels who thus sinned were consigned to Tartarus is revealed in the New Testament (2 Peter 2:4-9; Jude 1:6, 7), but the fate of their mongrel offspring is not told in Scripture.

Biblical interpretations

Demons are unconfined fallen angels. In view of the Bible's silence regarding the origin of demons, the best supported deduction from scriptural hints is that demons are fallen angels. When Lucifer rebelled and introduced sin into a previously sinless universe, he drew with him a great number of lower celestial beings (Matthew 25:41; Revelation 12:4). These demons are free to roam the heavens under their leader prince, who became Satan, also called "Beelzebub, prince of the demons" (Matthew 12:24), "Satan and his angels" (Matthew 25:41), and "the dragon . . . and his angels" (Revelation 12:7).

In Satan's kingdom and under his rule, demons are his subjects and helpers (Matthew 12:26). They are so numerous that Satan's power is practically ubiquitous. They are also so well organized that satanic strategy can use them as effectively as a commander-in-chief wielding a great army (Ephesians 6:11, 12).

Satan's abode and base of operation is not in hell, but in the heavenly realms — not, however, in the third heaven or heaven of heavens (2 Corinthians 12:2). There the ascended Christ is seated *"far above* all rule, and authority, and power, and dominion" (Ephesians 1:21). Satan was expelled from this *highest heaven,* evidently not at the time of his primeval fall (cf. Job 1:6), but after Christ completed his redemptive work and glorious ascension. As "prince of the power of the air" (Ephesians 2:2), Satan and his wicked minions are confined to the first and second heavens. During the great tribulation, Satan and his evil accomplices will be cast down to earth (Revelation 12:7-12), where they will make a last futile attempt to seize control of man and the earth (Revelation 19: 20; 20:2, 3).

Demons also include confined or imprisoned fallen angels. In addition to the hosts of demons who are at liberty and serve Satan in the heavenly spheres, multitudes are confined in the abyss (Luke 8:31; Revelation 9:2, 11). This is evidently a temporary prison for evil spirits, who are apparently too depraved and harmful to be allowed to roam upon the earth. However, after the Church has been glorified and removed from earth (1 Thessalonians 4:13-18; 2 Thessalonians 2:1-9), these vile spirits will be let loose to afflict and deceive wicked men who will follow Satan in the last demon-energized rebellion against God (Revelation 9:1-21; 16:13, 14; cf. 2 Thessalonians 2:8-10; Revelation 13:1-18).

Why these demons are imprisoned is not explained in Scripture. They were originally numbered among Satan's free hosts, who roam the heavens. Perhaps their loss of freedom was the divine penalty for possessing human beings to satisfy their illicit desires or to perpetrate especially heinous crimes. Perhaps their victims' suicide left them helplessly exposed to the abyss. Apparently demons expelled from possessed people were automatically confined to the prison of depraved spirits, as in the case of the Gadarene demoniac (Luke 8:31).

Scripture does reveal, however, that the angels who left their "first estate" are bound in "Tartarus" rather than in the "abyss" (2 Peter 2:4, 5; Jude 1:6). These are thought by many scholars[12] to be "the sons of God" (fallen angels or demons) who cohabited with mortal women, producing moral chaos in God's established order of created beings. Their crime was so enormous that these lawless spirits (demons) and perhaps their monstrous offspring, were punished with imprisonment in Tartarus, the Greek nether world, comparable to hades, rather than in the regular prison of demons — the abyss. The flood may have been another indication of the enormity of their crime, in which God destroyed the offspring of this bizarre union.

Are demons active today?

Evidence that demons exist prompts another question: Are demons interacting with our modern world of science and so-called enlightenment? Skepticism and ignorance concerning the Word of God produce appalling misapprehensions of reality. Men who deny the existence of Satan and demons betray their rejection of biblical teachings; people who deny the activity of demons in contemporary life betray their ignorance of significant portions of the Bible.

This is the plight of many liberal churchmen and of untrained Christians. They leave the safe moorings of the Word of God and are caught in swirling currents of occult fortune-telling, spiritism, magic, and false cults. A notable example is the late Bishop James A. Pike, who in September 1967 allegedly communicated in a televised séance with his deceased son (a suicide), through a well-known medium, Arthur Ford (now deceased), who was at the same time a Disciples of Christ minister.[13] This sensational séance startled people all over the world and alerted Bible students to the reality of modern occultism and traffic in demonism.[14]

The tragic picture today includes the well-meaning but ill-taught Christian who professes to believe and honor the Word of God. Such a Christian, through ignorance of what the Bible teaches, may näively become the victim of the fallacious reasoning that since God can heal and perform miracles, then every case of healing and everything that passes for a miracle is from God. In seeking to be healed or helped, Christians may become involved in some form of demon-energized magic.

Satan knows biblical terminology. He is also a master in masquerading under the guise of divine power. Alleged miraculous cures or manifestations often are accompanied by doctrinal errors. Every believer should realize that Satan can use doctrinal errors to his advantage, but he cannot overcome the

Christian's defenses in God's Holy Word! This is our bulwark against demon incursion.

In the measure that we neglect or abandon the Word of God, demonism flourishes. Ignorance of biblical truth breeds gullibility. Deception is easy when the Word of God is not taught accurately. We are ready to believe anything when we cannot evaluate it in the light of biblical truth (1 John 4:1-6).

The contemporary Church lacks awareness of its true spiritual dimension and power. As a result many are seeking spiritual direction and help from organizations that stress psychic phenomena and experiences, such as *The Religious Research Foundation of America* (RRFA), *The Association for Research and Enlightenment* (ARE), *Inner Peace Movement* (IPM), and *The Spiritual Frontiers Fellowship* (SFF).

Others are turning to the delusions of spiritualism and to fortune-tellers for guidance. They neglect the Bible and seek enlightenment and comfort in the literature of occultism and metaphysics. Books such as *A Gift of Prophecy: The Phenomenal Jeane Dixon; Edgar Cayce: The Sleeping Prophet; Nothing So Strange;* and *The Search for Bridey Murphy* have enjoyed a phenomenal sale. All types of metaphysical literature are inundating the market, especially books on astrology, the ancient, pseudoscientific art cultivated by King Nebuchadnezzar (Daniel 2:2).

Sales of horoscope magazines run into the millions. Monthly horoscope columns appear in prominent magazines such as *Cosmopolitan, Harper's Bazaar, Ladies Home Journal,* one being authored by Sybil Leek, self-styled as "the most famous witch in the world." Horoscope columns appear in over a thousand daily newspapers.

The scope and power of modern occultism staggers the imagination. Millions are unwittingly oppressed and enslaved by the occult. No wonder mental and emotional problems increase at an alarming rate. Unless the reality and purpose of Satan and demons are acknowledged, some of these problems will not be solved.

NOTES
CHAPTER 1

1. Baruch 4:7. That demonism is the dynamic of paganism is a clear revelation of Scripture (Psalm 95:5, Septuagint; 1 Corinthians 10:20).
2. George W. Gilmore, "Demon, Demoniac," *New Schaff-Herzog Encyclopedia of Religious Knowledge,* 3: 399.
3. T. Witton Davies, *Magic, Divination, and Demonology Among the Hebrews and Their Neighbors;* Taufik Canaan, *Demonenglaube im Lande der Bibel;* T. K. Oesterreich, *Possession, Demoniacal and Other Among Primitive Races in Antiquity, the Middle Ages, and Modern Times;* Walter Scott, *The Existence of Evil Spirits Proved.*
4. Davies, *Demonology Among the Hebrews,* p. 95.
5. L. T. Townsend, *Satan and Demons,* p. 43.
6. Father Delaporte, *The Devil: Does He Exist? And What Does He Do?,* pp. 13-16; Scott, *Evil Spirits Proved,* pp. 18, 19. For objections to the doctrines of evil angels answered, see Augustus Strong, *Systematic Theology,* pp. 460-464; Lewis Sperry Chafer, *Systematic Theology,* 1: 28-32, 37, 38.
7. Davies, p. 103.
8. Flavius Josephus, *Wars of the Jews,* 7. 6. 3.
9. G. H. Pember, *Earth's Earliest Ages and Their Connection with Modern Spiritualism and Theosophy,* pp. 72, 73.
10. Hesiod, *Works and Days,* trans. Richard Lattimore, pp. 109-126.
11. For a full discussion pro and con of this problem, see Merrill F. Unger, *Biblical Demonology,* 8th ed., pp. 45-52. W. F. Albright says that "the Israelites who heard this section recited unquestionably thought of intercourse between angels and women (like later Jews and Christians)" (*From the Stone Age to Christianity,* p. 226). For the role of Satan and demons in illicit sex see Brad Steiger, *Sex and Satanism,* pp. 73-97.
12. A. C. Gaebelein, *The Annotated Bible,* 4: 82, 83.
13. Hobart E. Freeman, *Deliverance from Occult Oppression and Subjection,* pp. 1, 2. See Jess Stearn, "Bishop Pike's Strange Séances," *This Week, The Baltimore Sun,* January 28, 1968.
14. See the author's study of modern spiritism as the revival of an ancient form of demonism in *Biblical Demonology,* pp. 143-164. Cf. P. D. Payne and L. J. Bendit, *Psychic Sense;* N. Blonsdon, *A Popular Dictionary of Spiritualism.*

Demons Against Men

B iblical teaching on demonology is lofty and chaste and strikingly in contrast to the excesses and superstitions of pagan systems and even the demonology of rabbinic Judaism.[1] As part of divine revelation, it should be free from the crudities as well as errors of nonbiblical systems. The Bible does not deal with the impractical or that which would merely satisfy human curiosity. Hence it is reticent on many questions concerning Satan and demons that have little or no bearing on human life and conduct.

For example, in the study of demonical origin and identity, scriptural reserve demonstrates that the practical consideration is not where the demons came from nor precisely who they are, but that they actually exist, they are depraved and malevolent, and the human race is the prime target of their evil designs.[2]

The Bible warns that demons are pernicious enemies of man and illustrates the tragic role they play in human experience. At the same time the Bible clearly outlines how men can be delivered from sin and evil supernaturalism through the redemptive work of Christ and the power of the Holy Spirit (Colossians 1:13; 2:15; Ephesians 6:10-18; 1 Peter 5:8; Revelation 12:11).

What are demons like?

The Bible is quite explicit regarding the nature of demons and the methods they use in tempting, deceiving, and enslaving human beings. Scripture acquaints us with our spiritual foes so that we may be delivered from their power and free to do the will of God.

Demons are spiritual beings

The Bible presents demons as spiritual beings or spirit personalities. The specific attribute of "spirit" is incorporeality or immateriality. "A spirit hath not flesh and bones" (Luke 24: 39); that is, demons do not possess a material body. On the other hand, they can act upon the human body, as well as the human soul and spirit. They are capable of entering in and assuming control of a human body, speaking and acting through it from time to time and even possessing it, as if it were their own property.

That demons are spirits is clear from numerous references in the Gospels. "When the even was come, they brought unto him many that were possessed with *demons*: and he cast out the *spirits* with his word" (Matthew 8:16). When the seventy returned and joyfully declared, "Lord, even the demons are subject unto us" (Luke 10:17), our Lord replied, "Nevertheless in this rejoice not, that the spirits are subject unto you" (v. 20). "The demon" who went out of the lunatic boy, as described in Matthew 17:18, is also called a "foul spirit" in Mark 9:25.

The Apostle Paul emphatically declares that Satan and his demons are spirits. In describing the believers' conflict against the powers of darkness, he indicates that the intense warfare "is not against flesh and blood" but against evil spirits, described as "principalities, powers, rulers of the darkness," and "spiritual hosts of wickedness in the heavenly places" (Ephesians 6:12).

The Apostle John also indicates that demons are spirits. He describes the three unclean spirits issuing from the mouth of the dragon, of the beast, and of the false prophet, as the "spirits of demons" (Revelation 16:14). The expression may be interpreted either as a common genitive of description, defining the spirits as "demonic," or better as a genitive of apposition, more particularly defining the general term "spirits," which may be either good or bad, as bad, or "demon-spirits."

Demons are personalities

The fact that demons are spirits, and thus immaterial and incorporeal, does not in the least suggest that they lack individuality, with all the elements of personality such as will, feelings, and intellect. Like all God's creatures, they were constituted with self-determining choice. Created originally sinless, they joined Satan in a chosen course of rebellion. Their decision was deliberate and in the full knowledge of the infinite goodness and holiness of their Creator. This is why they are incorrigible and confirmed in their depravity with no hope of repentance or change. Like Satan's, their choice is irretrievable; their doom is sealed (Luke 8:31; Revelation 20:1, 2, 10, 15).

That demons are individuals is attested by their intelligent and voluntary actions. They think, they speak, they act (Acts 19:15, 16) through a spiritistic medium or through a person over whom they have acquired control. In the case of the demon possessed, the domination is almost complete (Mark 5:10; Luke 4:34). In case of demon influence, their control is less complete and direct (1 Timothy 4:1, 2; 1 John 4:1, 2).

Because demons are spirit personalities, they can act upon and influence man's body and mind. Counselors, parapsychologists, and psychiatrists who deny or ignore this sphere of reality render themselves unequipped to deal with patients who may be suffering from occult oppression and subjection in a day when disturbances of both mind and body from this source are becoming more numerous and more pronounced.[3]

Demons are invisible

Divine revelation uniformly views demons or evil spirits as denizens of the world of evil supernaturalism operating above the natural law. Spirits are not normally subject to human visibility or other sensory perception. God's universe operates undeviatingly in accordance with the purpose for which he created it. The all-wise and all-powerful Creator is not permitting Satan and demons to throw his ordered universe into confusion by violating the laws he has established. Nor is he permitting his own people to do so through haphazard miracles.

Though not ignoring the laws of nature, God's Word also recognizes the possible transcendence of natural law in divine miracle both in good supernaturalism (Exodus 14:19-31; 17:5-7; Joshua 3:16, 17; 6:20; John 2:9; 11:44) and in evil supernaturalism (Exodus 7:10, 11, 22; 8:7; 2 Thessalonians 2:8-10; Revelation 13:15).

When natural law is transcended by divine miracle, the natural eye may see the spiritual reality. An illustration is provided in 2 Kings 6:17. In answer to Elisha's prayer, the Lord "opened the eyes" of the prophet's servant who saw "the mountain full of horses and chariots of fire round about Elisha." In like manner Elisha saw the "chariot of fire, and horses of fire" when Elijah went up by a whirlwind into heaven (2 Kings 2:11). Similarly John saw the demons coming up from the abyss in their last-day eruption as locusts (Revelation 9:1-12). He also saw the three hideous demons issuing from the mouths of the dragon, the beast, and the false prophet as froglike spirits (Revelation 16:13, 14).

The apocalyptic seer glimpsed these foul spirits prophetically and by supernatural vision. But when they are sent against men they will be invisible to the natural eye. Their presence will be known by the excruciating pain they inflict and the gross deception they cause. The harm they inflict will be inescapable, because their victims will be unable to shield themselves from an invisible enemy.

But spirits can become discernible to men through transcendence of natural law. Evil spirits may be seen and communicated with through an intermediary or medium. Just as Peter and Paul saw and talked with an angel (Acts 5:19; 27:23, 24), so human beings today can communicate with evil spirits through magic rites and incantations.

Communication with the demon world results in supernatural manifestations, but these, strictly speaking, are not miraculous. Occult enslavement and extrasensory phenomena await people who enter the realm from which God would protect his own people (Deuteronomy 18:10, 11) and against which he solemnly warns them (Leviticus 19:31; 20:27; 1 Samuel 28:9; 1 Timothy 4:1, 2; 1 John 4:1-3).

When men ignore God's warnings and enter a forbidden realm, they may witness materializations, levitations, and luminous apparitions, as well as experience spirit rappings, trances, automatic writing, magic phenomena, clairvoyance, oral and written communications and other forms of spiritistic phenomena. Such manifestations are not miracles. They represent the operation of the occult within a certain well-defined sphere tolerated by God. Occult subjection and oppression are the inevitable penalties to all who traffic in the realm of evil supernaturalism.[4]

The Scriptures are markedly reticent on the matter of spirits being seen by humans. Here again the Bible stands in contrast to ethnic and rabbinic systems. Multitudes of demons in bizarre forms are described in ancient semitic demonology.[5] Rabbinic demonology, for example, divides demons into two classes: one composed of purely spiritual beings, the other of half-spirits.[6] The latter were thought to have a psycho-sarcous constitution that involved them in physical needs and functions. Although the Bible is silent concerning such *"halbgeister,"* they would seem to be what the offspring of the angels and mortal women (Genesis 6:1-4) might have been, half-angelic and half-human monsters.

Demonic intelligence

Plato derived the etymology of the word "demon" (Greek, *daimon*) from an adjective meaning "intelligent" or "knowing." If this derivation is correct, it suggests that intelligence was considered a prominent characteristic of demons.[7] This would be expected, if demons are fallen angels. As Satan's vast wisdom became vitiated when he sinned (Ezekiel 28:12, 17), the great wisdom that characterizes angels in general (2 Samuel 14:20) must also have been corrupted in his followers. This is undoubtedly why demons use their great but perverted knowledge so relentlessly in an effort to frustrate God's purposes.

Men who consult professional mediums and use other methods of divination to obtain knowledge of the future seem to imply a degree of confidence in the intelligence of evil spirits. The superior knowledge demons possess is not a holy or saving knowledge. Demons "believe" but only to "tremble" (James 2:19). They are confirmed in depravity and never seek forgiveness. As preeminently unclean spirits, they never long for purity. They confess Jesus Christ is Lord, but they do not trust Christ or submit to him, although they recognize his authority (Mark 1:24; 5:6, 7). They cleverly withhold knowledge of his incarnation and completed redemption (1 John 4:1-6), corrupt sound doctrine (1 Timothy 4:1-3), discern between those who have God's seal and those who do not (Revelation 9:4), and know full well their own tragic destiny and inevitable doom (Matthew 8:29).

Demonic strength

Their superhuman intellect is accompanied by superphysical strength. The psalmist celebrates this angelic characteristic: "Bless the Lord, ye his angels, that excel in strength, that do his commandments, hearkening unto the voice of his word" (Psalm 103:20). The Apostle Peter also speaks of the "power and might" of angelic spirits (2 Peter 2:11). Our Lord himself indirectly referred to demonic strength (cf. Matthew 12:29).

Perverted power and strength are thus conspicuous attributes of fallen angels. This titanic energy is displayed in the supernatural strength demons can impart to the human body when they enter it and possess it. The Gadarene demoniac who was dominated by a "legion" of demons (Mark 5:9) could not be bound even with chains. "Because that he had been often bound with fetters and chains, and the chains had been plucked asunder by him, and the fetters broken in pieces: neither could any man tame him" (Mark 5:4).

The great strength of this demoniac was due to the vast number of demons who possessed him. "A legion" in Roman military history consisted of three to six thousand foot soldiers, and three to seven hundred cavalry. The term "legion" was not only the name of the possessed man but probably also served to indicate the phenomenal strength of the demoniac. The demons were so powerful that when the Lord ordered them to enter a herd of two thousand swine, they caused the entire herd to rush violently down a hill into the sea (Mark 5:13). No wonder the demon-possessed man was disturbed physically, mentally, and emotionally.

But the superphysical strength of demons is not limited to the physical energy they impart to their victim. Their power is broad enough to cause occult oppression of mind and body. They can produce physical disabilities and sicknesses unrelated to organic disorders and which medicine or natural therapy cannot alleviate.

Perhaps the most terrible power of demons is to derange the mind by upsetting the nervous system. In this way they can afflict the body with a psychosomatic disease. Demons are aware of the close relationship between physical and mental health.

By jangling the nerves and the emotions, they can cause mental instability (Luke 8:26-36), producing suicidal mania (Mark 9:22). Their purpose is to drive their occult-enslaved victims to self-destruction.

Demonic depravity

Although demons reveal various degrees of wickedness (Matthew 12:45), they all are depraved. This aspect of their character appears in the terrible things they do to their victims. The Bible often refers to them as spiritually and morally "unclean" (Matthew 10:1; Mark 1:27; 3:11; Luke 4:36; Acts 8:7; Revelation 16:13).

People who deal in the occult are often found to be immoral. Men and women who abandon themselves to immorality reach a point when God gives them up, in the sense of restraining Satan and demonic power from them, so that they are abandoned to the degrading depths of immorality and are shamelessly reduced to actions that even animals avoid (Romans 1: 26-32; cf. Revelation 9:20, 21).

In such moral decay the "unclean spirit" takes possession of the sinner to gratify his senses through every type of unclean pleasure. This is apparently why a demoniac often desires to live in a state of nudity and harbors licentious thoughts (Luke 8:27). When men disobey the moral laws of God, especially the law of loving and honoring their Creator, they choose the depraved way of Satan and demons.

What demons can do to men

The character of demons reveals what they can do to their victims. Invisible, extremely intelligent, strong, and totally depraved personalities can do a great deal of harm to the unregenerate person, leading him into evil (Ephesians 2:2, 3; Colossians 1:13). As believers it is good to know that God is for us and that Christ's victory is complete. He protects us from evil. The healthy Christian will never suffer from occult oppression.

Demons use men to oppose God

Satan's main occupation is opposition to God's will. The name "Satan," given Lucifer after his fall, means "adversary" — God's adversary (Job 1:6; Matthew 13:39), and man's, especially when man loves and serves God (Zechariah 3:1; 1 Peter 5:8). It was the intrusion of Satan's will against the divine will that introduced sin into a sinless universe and transformed "Lucifer" (Lightbearer) into "Satan" (Opposer). Satan's rebellion fixed the pattern of satanic and demonic attitude as opposition to God and exaltation of self. This demonic strategy was evident in Cain's murder of Abel (Genesis 4:8) and in Herod's slaughter of the innocents (Matthew 2:16). The evil one was seeking to slay the promised seed of the woman (Genesis 3:15) to prevent the incarnation of the Savior of the world, who would eventually seal the doom of Satan and the demons in Gehenna (Revelation 20:10-15).

When the Lord Jesus began his public ministry, Satan appeared in person to tempt him (Matthew 4:1-11). Christ's ministry on earth provoked an outburst of demonic activity. Demonic power incited Judas to betray Jesus, Peter to deny him (Luke 22:3, 31), and the leaders of the Jewish nation to reject and crucify him. The powers of darkness appear in early Church history as recorded in Acts (cf. Acts 4:25, 26; 5:3; 8:9; 13:6-13; 16:16-18; 19:11-20, etc.).

The opposition of Satan and his demons can be discerned in every era of church history. The unseen forces of evil will increase their activity in the latter times (1 Timothy 4:1; Revelation 9:1-21), culminating in the demon-inspired debacle at Armageddon (Revelation 16:13, 14). Not until Satan and his demons are confined to the abyss, the prison of evil spirits (Zechariah 13:2; Revelation 20:1-3), will the kingdom of righteousness and peace supplant the present satanic world system (1 John 2:17).

Demons can oppress the mind

Many mental and emotional illnesses are, of course, due to natural causes, such as overwork, tension, fatigue, malnutrition, organic diseases, etc. Such disorders can be treated effectively by a physician, neurologist, psychologist, or psychiatrist. Demonic spirits may have little or nothing to do with such disorders of the mind. The causes are purely natural and may be corrected by purely natural means. This is not surprising since the Creator has placed the creation and his creatures under the normal operation of the laws of cause and effect.

Since the supernatural exists and does interact with the natural world, the truly scientific investigator must take this into consideration. Prayer and faith can heal the mind and body supernaturally, just as medicine and rest can do it naturally. By the same token, unbelief and sin can harm body and mind as a result of demonic bondage.

Demons can influence the mind. Bondage to demonic forces can be of varying degrees, as can yieldedness to God and control by the Holy Spirit. The Bible clearly teaches that man exposed himself to evil powers through the fall (Genesis 3:15; 2 Corinthians 4:4; Colossians 1:13; Ephesians 6:10-20). Some unsaved people who live a balanced moral life are only mildly influenced by demonic spirits, while others, who flout God's moral laws, are severely influenced to the point of subjection. Others are so dominated that they are oppressed and tormented, and some are completely possessed by evil spirits.

When mental and emotional disturbances are due almost entirely to natural causes, medical and psychological care can be very successful. But when demonic influence, however slight, is at work, complete healing can only be achieved with the help of God through Christ. Successful therapy could be used if all psychologists, psychiatrists, counselors, and physicians were Christians with a knowledge of the gospel of deliverance from sin and Satan.[8]

When demonic influence is mild, it is almost impossible to distinguish between natural and supernatural causes. Only treatment that deals with the full gamut of causes will solve all the problems and insure a full cure. Parapsychology, which deals with extraordinary phenomena, will never fully understand these cases, much less effect deliverance, until the demonic factor is recognized and dealt with accordingly.

Demons can subject the mind. Demon subjection is one step beyond demon influence. When the moral law of God is persistently and flagrantly disregarded, demon influence may merge into demon subjection. The sinner then becomes the slave of the demon. Those who commit adultery and yield themselves to fornication and sexual excesses become slaves of illicit lust, perhaps goaded on by vile spirits that master their victims and drive them on to moral ruin. Those who nurse hate and revenge may find that a superhuman power takes over, impelling them to murder. Those who covet become slaves of greed. Those who persistently lie may become enslaved by an evil spirit of falsehood until they are incapable of telling the truth. Persistent sin against the second table of the moral law regulating man's conduct toward man (Exodus 20:13-17) opens the door to demon power that can derange man's mind, weaken his will, alienate his affections, and disturb his emotions.

But persistent, flagrant sin against the first table of the law regulating man's conduct toward God, especially the first commandment prohibiting idolatry (Exodus 20:3-5), leads to occultism and results in God's curse. The dynamic of idolatry is demonism since idolatry is in reality the worship of other gods who are demons (1 Corinthians 10:20), headed by Satan, the "god of this world" (2 Corinthians 4:4). Occultism involves dealing with demonic forces through fortune-telling, magic, spiritism, or fake religious cults, which are closely allied to idolatry.

Persons who deal in the occult often discover that they have spiritistic sensitivity, extrasensory perception, or abnormal intellectual powers enabling them to engage in clairvoyance, precognition, divination, psychometry, magic, and spiritism.

Dealing in the occult often results in subjection to the powers of darkness to such a degree that the mind becomes blinded to truth, immersed in deception and error. This frequently results in acute depression with thoughts of self-destruction. However, not all emotional problems or suicidal tendencies should be attributed to occultism.

Demons can oppress the human mind. Enslavement to demons sometimes reaches a point in which the demonic spirits harass and torment their victims. In the preceding stage of subjection, the evil spirits sporadically dominate their victims, but they do not necessarily harass them, at least not as they do in this deeper and more tragic state of oppression. Oppression in some form will be the final outcome of all who become psychically enslaved, even though some are not psychically gifted with spiritistic or magical powers.

One well-attested and widely occurring form of demonic oppression is *poltergeist phenomena.* "Poltergeist" is German for "noisy ghost." In such a case, the oppressed person is hounded by strange noises and sounds, such as shouts and obscene threats, rattling of chains, moaning, weeping, or piercing laughter. Dishes clatter, furniture is moved by invisible hands, and myriads of other strange happenings occur, invisibly produced by spirits connected with a haunted house where spiritistic activity has been practiced. Some who are oppressed continue to be tormented even though they may move to another residence.[9] The author has counseled with psychically disturbed people troubled with strange noises.

Also common in the victims of demonism are the appearances of ghosts, specters and monstrous phantasms. These phenomena are often explained away as hallucinations, but are well attested in occultism as spirits appearing as dwarfs, animals, dismembered parts of a human body, etc.[10] At times these hideous spirits will choke, bite, strike, or attack their victims in some way.

Perhaps the most terrible and revolting form of demonic oppression is what is known in the history of religion as incubi and succubae experiences. This is the assault by an unclean spirit upon its enslaved victim for the purpose of sexual lust. Both men and women have been attacked and molested by "seducing male and female demons."[11] Such fully established phenomena show that angelic-human union, a major cause of the flood (Genesis 6:1-4; cf. 2 Peter 2:4; Jude 1:6, 7), has its parallel in occultism today.

Demons can oppress the body

Demons can cause physical ailments such as dumbness (Matthew 9:32, 33), blindness (Matthew 12:22), and various other defects and deformities (Luke 13:11-17). In all such cases medical and psychiatric treatment are of no avail, because the cause is demonic. Only by dealing with the spiritual cause of the malady can it be cured.

Beside actual sickness, demons can cause speech and behavior abnormalities.[12] In demon possession, which is an extreme form of enslavement and oppression, the speech and behavior abnormalities appear in greatly accentuated form with such violent physical manifestations as retching, screaming, blaspheming, cursing, foaming at the mouth, convulsions and display of tremendous physical strength. So completely does the demonic spirit gain mastery that he takes over the body of the victim and speaks through it with his own voice and language, which may be completely foreign to the language of the demonized.[13]

Demons alienate men from God

Cult involvement steels the unbeliever against the gospel, causing him to resist the Word of God and hardening him in unbelief and rebellion. In the case of nominal Christians, occult complicity produces a deadly indifference to the Word of God, prayer, worship, and spiritual life in general. This condition develops against the will of the victim who cannot overcome his spiritual apathy. At the same time, the victim is open to other religious delusions and heresies, being insensitive to the stern warnings of God's Word against complicity in the occult (Deuteronomy 18:9, 10). Opposition to God becomes violent and complete apostasy inevitably results with "doctrines of demons" and the denial of Christ's deity (1 Timothy 4:1, 2; 1 John 2:1-3).

Demons hinder man's general well being

Under their leader, the arch-tempter Satan, demons subject man to temptations (Genesis 3:1-7; Matthew 4:3; John 13:27, Acts 5:3; 1 Thessalonians 3:5). Satanic and demonic solicitations are both negative and positive (Matthew 13:38, 39). Satan and his helpers not only destroy the good seed in men's hearts; they sow bad seed.

Sometimes evil spirits endanger man's temporal safety by exercising a certain control over natural forces. Satan employed lightning, whirlwind, and disease to afflict Job (Job 1:12, 16, 19; 2:7). The woman in a weakened condition had been held in bondage by Satan for eighteen years (Luke 13:11, 16).

The demons' primary objective is to destroy peace and harmony and to introduce as much anguish, grief, misfortune, privation, suspicion, anxiety, and confusion as possible into human life.

God is still sovereign

God is sovereign and in perfect control of the universe. His plan will prevail in spite of satanic opposition. God uses demons to punish the ungodly (Psalm 78:49), as in the case of wicked Ahab at Ramoth-gilead (1 Kings 22:23) and the God-defying armies at Armageddon (Revelation 16:13, 14).

God also uses demons to chasten the godly. In Peter's case, the Lord used Satan's sifting to separate truth from falsehood (Luke 22:31). Job was refined in his furnace of satanic testing (Job 42:5, 6). The immoral Corinthian believer was delivered to Satan for physical death that he might be preserved for spiritual and eternal life (1 Corinthians 5:5).

Through the career of Satan, demons, and fallen men, God is demonstrating to all the universe the nature and end of moral evil (Matthew 8:29). Demonic doom in the lake of fire (Matthew 25:41; Revelation 20:10-15) will both vindicate God's tolerance of the demons' evil career and demonstrate before all created beings the exceeding sinfulness of sin and its inevitable punishment.

NOTES
CHAPTER 2

1. For a comparison see Merrill F. Unger, *Biblical Demonology*, 8th ed., pp. 21-34. Cf. Louis M. Sweet, "New Testament Demonology," *International Standard Bible Encyclopedia*, 2: 828; G. Edward Langton, *Essentials of Demonology*, pp. 20-22.
2. Cf. Charles Hodge, *Systematic Theology*, 2: 28-32, 37, 38; Rob-

ert Penn-Lewis and Evan Roberts, *War on the Saints,* pp. 16, 17.
3. See Hobart E. Freeman, *Deliverance from Occult Oppression and Subjection,* pp. 1-63; Kurt E. Koch, *Between Christ and Satan,* p. 9.
4. Kurt E. Koch, *Christian Counseling and Occultism,* trans. Andrew Petter, p. 162.
5. Langton, *Essentials of Demonology,* pp. 20-22; R. Campbell Thompson, *Semitic Magic,* pp. 44, 57, 60, 62.
6. Cf. William M. Alexander, *Demonic Possessions in the New Testament,* pp. 25, 26.
7. Cratylus 1. 389. On the intellectual nature of demons see Langton, pp. 153, 170; John L. Nevius, *Demon Possession and Allied Themes,* 5th ed., pp. 33, 83, 150, 296.
8. Cf. Koch, *Christian Counseling,* pp. 256-261.
9. Freeman, p. 40; Koch, *Christian Counseling,* pp. 144-153; Koch, *Between Christ and Satan,* pp. 136-140.
10. Koch, *Between Christ and Satan,* pp. 144-149.
11. Koch, *Christian Counseling,* p. 134.
12. Freeman, pp. 44, 45.
13. For a discussion on demon possession see Unger, *Biblical Demonology,* 8th ed., pp. 77-106. See also chapter 3.

Demons and Spiritism

Spiritism is defined by Rudolf Tischner as "a spiritual activity, grounded in the persuasion that people can by means of certain persons, certain mediums, make contact with the deceased, and so acquire revelations from the beyond."[1] This endeavor to communicate with the dead in the spirit world is called "spiritualism" by certain groups who scorn contact with vile spirits and label it "spiritism." No matter what it's called, God's Word severely condemns and prohibits such communication (Leviticus 19:31; 20:27; Deuteronomy 18:9, 10). Traffic in spiritism always results in bondage to occult powers, instead of producing fellowship with God. It leads to a false spirituality which not only deceives but enslaves.

Spiritism can be traced from the most ancient times. The Noahic flood, in fact, was a necessary divine judgment upon a civilization that had sunk to the lowest levels of immorality and violence because of dealings in the occult and consequent moral corruption (Genesis 6:1-4, 11, 13). Occultism is the dynamic of idolatry (1 Corinthians 10:20). The Israelite nation was born and lived in a world that was honeycombed with spiritism (1 Samuel 28:3-25). It posed a constant threat of contamination to the Lord's people.

The great non-Christian religions, both of ancient and modern times, "to a large extent are spiritistically oriented."[2] Occultism has also played a prominent role in the history of Christianity. This will be climaxed by a tremendous outburst of evil toward the end of the Church era (1 Timothy 4:1). The ensuing demon-inspired apostasy and revolt will precipitate Christ's second advent in glory and the consignment of

Satan and demons to the abyss (the demon prison), to open the way for the establishment of God's kingdom on earth (Revelation 19:1—20:3).

The phenomena of spiritism

If spiritism pertained only to pagan religions and had never affected the people in so-called Christian lands, then a careful study of its practices and phenomena might not be imperative. Interest in the occult is reaching alarming proportions and even some professing Christians are being duped into complicity with spiritistic traffic. This was true of the late Bishop James A. Pike, as reported in a preceding chapter.

Worldwide spiritism is conservatively estimated to have at least seventy million adherents. Kurt E. Koch, a German evangelist and student of the occult for thirty years, enumerates sixteen different varieties of spiritistic practices. All of these must be carefully understood if spiritism is to be accurately evaluated and its somber relation to human experience comprehended.[3]

Spiritistic phenomena may be conveniently divided into the following categories: 1. *physical phenomena,* (levitations, apports, and telekinesis); 2. *psychic phenomena* (spiritistic visions, automatic writing, speaking in a trance, materializations, table lifting, tumbler moving, excursions of the psyche); 3. *metaphysical phenomena* (apparitions, ghosts); 4. *magic phenomena* (magic persecution, magic defense); 5. *cultic phenomena* (spiritistic cults, spiritism among Christians.)

Physical phenomena

In the case of levitations, apports, and telekinesis, God allows the physical and natural laws of the universe to be superseded temporarily and in a restricted sense by higher laws of the spirit world. These phenomena are diabolical miracles (Exodus 7:22; 8:7; 2 Thessalonians 2:8-10; Revelation 13:14,

15), in distinction to divine miracles. Diabolical miracles are supernatural acts that imitate the power and benevolence of divine miracles.

It is as if God said to the powers of darkness what he said to the sea in the day of creation: "Hitherto shalt thou come but no farther, and here shall thy proud waves be stayed" (Job 38: 11). The demonic powers are allowed only a very small intrusion into the orderly realm of nature, and the miracles they produce are characterized by a rigid sameness. Everywhere in the domain of occultism there are reminders of God's absolute sovereignty. He is in majestic control. Demonic power makes such a poor show by its severe restrictions and drab sameness, that it actually advertises the glory of God for those who can see evil supernaturalism in the proper focus of divine revelation.

Levitations. Levitations (from the Latin verb *levito,* "to raise or lift") are objects or people that are raised up and appear floating in the air. Such phenomena are frequently reported in occult literature and experience, especially in connection with haunted houses, where strongly psychic people have lived and died, or where spiritistic séances have been held. Objects on occasion sail through the air as if thrown by an invisible hand, or spooks (ghosts) appear hovering in space. Furniture is lifted, often when a strong medium is present.[4] "Men, either in a conscious or unconscious state," are included in the phenomenon of levitation.[5]

Apports. The word "apport" (from the Latin *apportare,* "to carry away," "fetch") refers to the transference of objects through closed rooms and sealed containers by means of the penetration of matter. The phenomenon transcends the physical law that one solid cannot pass through another solid in the unchanged solid state. Kurt Koch cites an illustration of this phenomenon in a haunted farm house in the Swiss Alps. Objects appeared and disappeared in closed rooms and containers. Associated with these apports were other physical phenomena of spiritism such as levitations.

A committee consisting of a professor, an electrical engineer, and a philologist who was conversant with parapsychological phenomena, was delegated to examine the strange events in this haunted house. Their research disclosed that the fourteen-year-old son of the house was a strong spiritistic medium. "In the presence of the three-man team he accomplished some astonishing telekinetic feats. The highlight of his performance was the lifting and moving of his bed. This levitation phenomenon was repeated many times. The bed was also lifted up when the three men tried with all of their strength to keep it down."[6]

The penetration of matter by both good and evil spirits is illustrated by the glorified or spiritual human body. Our Lord's glorified, resurrection body passed through a sealed rock tomb before the angel rolled the stone away to show the empty tomb to his wavering and doubting disciples. In his glorified, resurrection body, our Lord could pass through closed doors and barred windows and appear to his disciples (John 20:19). When the believer's body is glorified at the rapture, it will be caught up instantly, whether from a closed airplane cabin or from the depths of a cave. Solid intervening matter will then no longer be a barrier, because the spiritual — yet evidently still a material substance, "flesh and bones" (Luke 24:37-41) — will no longer be bound by the physical laws of nature (cf. 1 Thessalonians 4:17; 1 Corinthians 15:51-53).

Telekinesis. This is the phenomenon that occurs when an object is set in motion without a visible or tangible cause (from the Greek, *tele,* a prefix meaning "far, operating at a distance" and *kinein* "to move"). This manifestation results in objects being caused to move mysteriously about a room or musical instruments to be played by unseen hands. Also in this category are such well-known phenomena of spiritistic practice as table lifting and tumbler moving at séances.

Although occult literature is full of examples of table lifting, this form of spiritistic practice has found many critics and detractors who do not take into account the reality of demon spirits and claim it is accomplished only by clever mechanical means.[7] But proof is found in the settings of the German physicist, Professor Zollner, with the American spiritist, Dr. Slade, a medical doctor. Slade's levitations and apport-phenomena were amazing and incontrovertible and could not be unmasked as impostures in spite of the best checks and scientific controls.[8]

Psychic phenomena

The physical phenomena of spiritism are often closely connected with psychical manifestations, such as spiritistic visions, automatic writing, speaking in a trance, materializations, table lifting, tumbler moving and excursions of the psyche. Christian psychiatrists and pastor-counselors need to be especially well informed in this field to help those who are occultly enslaved or oppressed.

Spiritistic visions. There is no doubt that today, as in the time of Isaiah (Isaiah 6:1-5), Ezekiel (Ezekiel 1:4-28), Paul (Acts 9:1-8), Peter (Acts 10:9-16), and John (Revelation 1: 10-18), God may give his people a genuine vision, particularly in times of great stress. But genuine experiences of this nature are always accompanied by true spiritual grace and modesty. Sensationalism betrays a lack of authenticity.

Unfortunately, genuine experiences are rare, and counterfeit ones abound. Christian counselors find that the "ratio is about nine to one over the genuine experiences."[9]

Dr. Koch counseled with a young theological student who reported that visions of Christ at night had left him with a sense of uneasiness and fear. It was discovered that both his mother and grandmother were spiritists and practiced glass-moving. This made it clear that the so-called visions of Christ were mediumistic and not produced by the Holy Spirit.[10]

The same evaluation must also be made of Diane Kennedy Pike's highly publicized vision of the departure of her husband's spirit from his body as he expired in the Judean desert in September 1969 and as he blissfully ascended to embrace his deceased son, Jim, Paul Tillich and others.[11] That this vision is mediumistic and not attributable to the Holy Spirit is evidenced by the thoroughly spiritistic context of the search for the bishop's body and his subsequent death.

The visions of Emanuel Swedenborg (1688-1772), who fostered the Swedenborgian heresy,[12] bear evidence of the occult, as do the visions of Joseph Smith (1805-1844), who fathered Mormonism. Many of the founders and promulgators of modern cults have had alleged visions from God. Since such sects distort biblical truth, it is doubtful that the visions were inspired by the Holy Spirit. Spiritistic visions promote "doctrines of demons" (1 Timothy 4:1) among the credulous and those unable to discern spirits (1 Corinthians 12:10; 1 John 4:1, 2). When men depart from God's Word, they expose themselves to demon imposture and deception.

Automatic writing. Some persons endowed with mediumistic powers are able — either in a waking state or a trance to write letters, words, or sentences which spiritists consider to be messages from the spirit world. Dr. Koch recounts the experience of a simple farm woman who discovered that a persistent pain in her lower right arm vanished whenever she sat down and wrote letters. After resorting to this method for relief, she soon developed a writing compulsion. She was penning something in the nature of a theological treatise, which astonished her pastor when she showed it to him.

One day as she wrote, a spirit named Felix appeared and said, "In the name of the Lord Jesus, our blessed and exalted Savior." The spirit then told the woman that she had been chosen by God for special revelations. She would become a prophetess and bless mankind with these revelations. The case is patently that of a simple farm woman turned indeed into a spiritistic writing medium.[13]

Rudolf Tischner, a parapsychologist, points out the danger of automatic writing when practiced in immoderation.[14] Although he regards these writing phenomena only as "motoric automatisms,"[15] he admits that they can enslave a person and break up the integrated psychic structure with ensuing peril to mental and psychical health. This simply means that occult enslavement can result from mediumistic writing, or from dependence upon the Ouija board or other spiritistic devices to obtain alleged messages from the spirit world.

Speaking in a trance. A trance is a condition in which a spiritistic medium loses consciousness and passes under the control of demonic power to effect alleged communication with the dead. The demon (or demons) takes over and actually speaks through the spiritistic medium, deceptively imitating the deceased. As a result of this ruse innumerable spiritistic clairvoyants claim communication with the dead, often with famous deceased people allegedly appearing to speak to the living.

A Protestant minister once participated in a séance with the purpose of examining a medium. The medium went into a trance and soon the "Apostle Paul" approached and preached to the audience. The apostle was not visible but only spoke through the medium who lay in a trance.

The minister followed the sermon of the alleged apostle with the greatest interest, but was disappointed in the banal content, consisting of a few moral statements with a Christian dressing. His evaluation was that the Apostle Paul had nothing to do with the performance, but that it was a case of unconscious fraud. It was just another common instance of deception by demons who can ape the deceased but cannot produce them.[16]

Materializations. Perhaps the most remarkable phenomena of spiritism are materializations. These are supernatural appearances and disappearances of material images in connection with the activities of a spiritistic medium. Materializations have been exhaustively studied and photographed and have been found to be manifestations of various degrees of teleplastic morphogenesis. The first stage is the evolution of a gauze-like substance of rubbery consistency from the body cavities of the medium.[17] The second stage is the forming of the various parts of the body in outline — arms, head, etc. Frequently in the case of teleplastic forms of this kind, a threadlike connection is maintained with the medium.[18]

The third stage consists of the composition into completely outlined forms, which are visible as phantoms near the medium. These three stages of materialization manifest purely visual phenomena. The fourth stage displays telekinetic phenomena. There is an energy output from the teleplasm (telekinesis), such as the ringing of a bell, automatic writing of a typewriter, and the automatic playing of a musical instrument. In addition to the active energy output of the materialization, there is frequently a passive pain experience of the teleplasm.

The fifth stage of the materialization is the penetration of material substance. To this phase belong "apports," that is, the appearing and disappearing of objects in closed rooms or chests and containers. From locked and cemented containers, for example, enclosed coins are brought out, or stones and other objects fall inexplicably from a ceiling.[19] In this stage many mediums allegedly have the ability to penetrate solid material substance while they are in a trance.

Larsen[20] relates the following results of twelve sessions with the celebrated medium, Madame D'Esperance. While the medium sat in a small cabinet, a phantom built itself up on the floor outside the cabinet and formed itself into a female person, who moved in and out among the participants of the séance. While the materialization extended her hand to one of those present and he held it, dematerialization began to occur before the eyes of all the participants. Soon there was only a lump on the floor and this rolled into the cabinet.

Another example is the medium who was assigned the task of calling and materializing the spirit of the deceased German romantic poet, Johann Ludwig Uhland (1787-1862). At the memorable séance a white phantasm was seen, from which the audience demanded a poem. Instead of reciting a poem, the phantasm tore a page from a book in the library. With a pencil from a briefcase in the room, secured through the leather without opening the briefcase, the hand jotted down a few verses and vanished. The page was left and still exists. Uhland experts immediately searched among the poet's works for this poem, but could not find it. The examination of the mysterious writing by a graphologist proved to be sensational. He confirmed the ghost writing to be actually the handwriting of the deceased poet. Afterward there was a trial in Berlin over the ownership of the page. The court awarded it to the medium, who afterward kept it among her prized possessions.[21]

The phenomena of materialization and dematerialization in the case of strong mediums illustrate the conversion of psychic energy into matter and matter changed back again into psychic energy. The problem is illustrated by nuclear physics. Einstein's formula ($E=Mc^2$), energy is equal to mass times the speed of light squared, simply declares that it is theoretically possible to convert energy to mass and back again to energy.

We have historical evidence of materializations. Missionaries claim that pagan priests in Japan dematerialize themselves on one mountain and rematerialize themselves on another mountain. This is to be regarded as a miracle of Satan (cf. 2 Thessalonians 2:8-10; Revelation 13:15). The case of Philip transported by the Spirit of God from Gaza to Azótus, twenty-five miles away (Acts 8:39, 40), may have been an example of this phenomenon or simply a miracle of transportation of his unaltered physical body. In any case, the New Testament recognizes both the miracle of God and that of Satan.

Table lifting. This common occurrence has been discussed at the beginning of this chapter. Table lifting is practiced by many spiritists under the delusion that it might help establish communication with the deceased or answer questions by the way the table turns or leans.

Martensen Larsen[22] relates how the physicist Barret, who was extremely skeptical of the phenomenon of telekinesis, overcame all doubts after a series of experiments. The physicist describes one of his experiences in the following words: "I had occasion to hold a . . . meeting. The room was brightly illuminated and after various tap-sounds had spelled out a message, a small table came, with no one touching it, hopping across the floor toward me until it completely barred me in my armchair. There were no threads or guides, or other accounting for these movements of the table."

In Tibet, where demon-controlled religion has resisted Christian missions, priests of the Taschi Lama possess tremendous occult gifts and are reported able to make tables fly through the air for a space of one hundred feet.[23] Above all, the so-called red-hooded monks are extremely adept in telekinesis, materialization, levitation, and black magic. Where Satan's power remains virtually unchecked, miracles of evil supernaturalism abound.

Tumbler moving. Spiritistic séances frequently use drinking glasses moved by telekinesis to spell out a message. A Christian minister, desiring to investigate this spiritistic phenomenon, took part in a series of séances. He relates that the participants sat around a table on which the letters of the alphabet were spread. The table was covered by glass on which stood a liquor goblet. After a ritualistic prayer, the spirit was invoked. The participants then asked questions of the invisible spirit. The answer was determined by the liquor glass moving about and coming to rest on single letters.

The powers behind these manifestations were no doubt demonic, since participation in these spiritistic sessions had grave repercussions for the minister. His interest in prayer and the ministry of God's Word faded away. On Sundays he faced terrible psychic assaults when he conducted worship service and attempted to preach. So intensified did this demonic oppression become that he was compelled to give up the ministry.[24]

Excursions of the psyche. Certain psychic clairvoyants claim that their souls can travel great distances at their command. The Lapps in Scandinavia and especially the Tibetans are known for the ability of soul excursion.

The following instance of psychic excursion stems from World War II. A German mother who had two sons missing on the Russian front took their respective photographs to a clairvoyant. Concentrating on the photographs, the medium declared that one son was apparently dead while the other one, reportedly killed in 1943, was still alive. After more concentration, the clairvoyant said: "I can get in touch with this son. I see him in a great stone building southeast of Moscow. He will return as a prisoner of war in 1954."

Lacking faith in the clairvoyant's prediction, the mother was all the more surprised when her son actually returned as a prisoner of war in early 1954. He had indeed been interned in a white stone building. By psychic excursion and by psychometry (selecting an object belonging to the missing person and beginning to search from there) the clairvoyant was able to establish contact by occult assistance.[25]

Metaphysical phenomena

This category lists apparitions and ghosts. Mere hallucinations, due to physical and psychological causes and curable through medical or psychiatric treatment, should be ruled out. Real apparitions and ghost phenomena can be objectively verified by any normal person. The objective apparition or ghost can be observed by persons or animals and photographed.

Those who attempt to explain apparitions and ghosts frequently resort to the metaphysical. According to spiritism, man not only leaves his body on earth at death but is a spiritual complex which keeps on existing independently in the astral world. Scripture gives no support to this theory but links these phenomena to the deceptive powers of darkness.

Apparitions. An apparition (from the Latin *apparere,* "to attend, appear") is a vision of a spirit in a strange or wonderful and often horrible form. It is sometimes called a specter. A pious, elderly widow became unduly concerned about her dead husband's eternal state. He had been a drunkard and an unbeliever. Prayer to God that she might see her husband in a dream brought no results, but a strange woman came to see her and told her that she could fulfill her desire. A visit to this woman resulted in the wall of the room becoming brightly lit. In the light-field the deceased man appeared with a horrible face, seated on a goat riding toward her. The widow was horribly terrified and renounced the desire ever to see her husband again.[26] However, from that time on, she became psychically oppressed with suicidal thoughts and a great antipathy toward anything spiritual. This clearly attests that the apparition was caused by demonic power. The woman consulted proved to be a notorious medium and leader of a spiritist group.

Occult literature is full of apparitions and specters. Jung-Stilling tells of a haunted house which for three centuries was continually disturbed by a nocturnal house-spirit. At night heavy steps were heard as of one carrying a heavy load. On occasion a form appeared in a monk's cowl.[27]

Locality-confined ghosts. These are spirits that plague a

so-called "haunted house." Prominent in occult literature also are "stable spooks" that plague cattle.[28] In all these cases some occult involvement or recourse to a conjurer or magician can be traced. The history of a haunted house usually reveals the practice of spiritistic phenomena. Certain ghosts are confined to certain places and plague certain people. They can be driven away only by prayer.

Magic phenomena

The wide scope of occult power possessed by spiritists helps explain why they can cause so much mischief. Through the phenomena of levitation, apports, telekinesis, and materializations, it is not difficult to see how a person endowed with strong mediumistic powers can do a great deal of harm, especially in the closely associated realm of magic.

Magic persecution. Genuine magic is the art of bringing about results beyond man's power through the enlistment of supernatural agencies. Black magic deliberately involves the devil and demons, and the resulting enchantment is used for persecution and revenge. A spiritistic circle of twenty members furnishes a good example. Working with black magic, these spiritists experimented to see if they could cause psychic harm or even illness in people they disliked. A strong medium of this occult group chose a minister as a target and vowed to afflict and eliminate him. The minister suffered a nervous breakdown and was unable to work for several months.[29]

Some phenomena must be eliminated from the spiritistic-magic field. In the psychiatric realm, for example, many schizophrenics claim to be magically persecuted. In reality this is only a symptom in the course of psychotic disease. Eliminating all such cases, there are still large-scale, genuine phenomena, especially in areas where occultism has flourished for many years.

One common form of magic persecution is beatings by an invisible attacker. Parapsychology also sees magical persecution as a mediumistic problem in the sphere of materializations.

Strong mediums (when under demon control) send out energy with which to build up human phantasms and are also able to transform this energy into animal forms, including dogs, cats, frogs, snakes, or human bodies with animal heads, etc. This explains the bizarre spiritistic persecution through phantoms in the form of various animals or human bodies with nonhuman heads. These animals bite, scratch, or otherwise torment their victims.

Examples of these occult phenomena abound in areas where the black arts are practiced. But such occurrences are denied by many intellectuals. Often peasants and country people, especially in Europe, know more about magic than university graduates, who claim swindle or hocus-pocus trickery are used instead of occult powers.

Magic defense. Magic defense enlists supernatural agencies to counteract or undo the mischief wrought by magic persecution. Various kinds of spells, charms, or incantations are employed. In spiritistic séances it is an established fact that injuries inflicted upon a phantasm are sustained by the medium, even in the case of animal phantasms. Many defensive customs developed to combat this threat since magic persecution involves materialization. If a victim can injure an aggressive phantasm he has won the struggle.

Cultic phenomena

When the rich man in Jesus' story asked for a messenger from the dead, the reply was, "They have Moses and the prophets" (i.e., the Word of God — Luke 16:29). The expansion of spiritism into a religious cult under the name "spiritualist" is without doubt the most dangerous form of this movement. Because of widespread departure from the Word of God, näive people are being blinded and confused by the Christian facade of such cults.

Spiritistic cults. Spiritism deceptively parades under the Christian banner in practically all civilized countries. A typical meeting consists of hymns, prayer, and a sermon as in a

Christian service. The sermon, however, is allegedly given by a spirit from the other world, through a medium, and denies cardinal Christian truths under a veneer of Christian moral precepts.

Spiritism among Christians. But spiritism and spiritistic phenomena are not confined to so-called spiritualist churches. The prominent Christian cults are affected by "doctrines of demons" to the extent that they stray from God's Word and press into the supernatural realm (1 Timothy 4:1; 1 John 4: 1-6). Even born-again Christians often cannot differentiate between the spiritual and the psychic-demonic when under the spell of doctrinal errors, particularly those concerning the work of the Holy Spirit. The result is confusion, division, and promotion of certain spiritual gifts contrary to the teaching of God's Word (1 Corinthians 13:8).

How is spiritism to be judged?

Lack of ability to discern spirits (cf. 1 Corinthians 10:12), which exists to a wide degree among Christians in an occult era, calls for a clear and unequivocal appraisal of all spiritistic phenomena.

The voice of science. Both psychiatry and psychology recognize the adverse effects of spiritistic activity upon the mind. Symptoms of split personality appear after sustained dealings in the occult. Psychiatry defines the resulting disorder as mediumistic psychosis. The German psychologist, Professor Hans Bender of the University of Freiburg, writes, "I have seen quite a number of patients who have suffered serious psychic disturbances through the misuse of such practices. They have become split personalities. The spirits which they called, confused them. He who tries to discover the promises of the other side through superstition endangers himself to fall a prey to the dark side of his psyche."[30]

The voice of Scripture. The Bible bans all spiritistic traffic. The medium and the clairvoyant are outlawed. "A man also or a woman that hath a familiar spirit (literally, 'in whom there is a divining demon') or that is a wizard (clairvoyant), shall surely be put to death . . . their blood shall be upon them" (Leviticus 20:27; cf. also Leviticus 19:31; 20:6; Deuteronomy 18:10, 11). The occult phenomena of the Old Testament have their roots in idolatry and are the result of worshiping other gods (demons) instead of the one true God (Exodus 20:3-5). The New Testament regards Old Testament occult phenomena as evidence of Satan's opposition to God's kingdom. Satan's kingdom of evil is doomed to eternal separation from God in a sin-cleansed universe.

Saul's visit to the spiritistic medium at Endor (1 Samuel 28: 3-25) is Scripture's exposé of the fraudulence of spiritism and its unequivocal condemnation of all complicity with occultism. Samuel's spirit was actually brought back from the spirit world, not by the medium of Endor, but by God himself. The Lord stepped in to show the duplicity of the spiritistic claim of communicating with the dead. The real appearance of Samuel so frightened the medium that she screamed out in fright, a sign that God had stepped in to expose the fraud.[31]

The voice of experience. Human experience corroborates scriptural revelation that spiritistic activity is demonic. He who dabbles in spiritism falls under the pall of psychic enslavement and deception! Experience also shows how utterly destructive spiritism can be to the life of the Christian.

Christians who attend séances or expose themselves to occult powers not only lose interest in spiritual things but become opposed to the truth of God. Ministers and lay workers who have dabbled in spiritism have experienced demon opposition to such a degree that they have often been compelled to give up their Christian work.[32] Many become enslaved and oppressed by occult powers and become victims of various manifestations of spiritistic phenomena.[33]

While overwhelming evidence from Christian counseling confirms the fact that spiritistic complicity seriously damages the believer's spiritual life, adherents of Buddhism, Islam, or even false cults of Christianity sense no ill effects. This was dramatically illustrated and brought to the attention of the world by the errant career of the late Episcopalian bishop,

James A. Pike. The reason is obvious. These religions fit the biblical category of "doctrines of demons," and are spiritistically oriented. Spiritism immunizes against the Holy Spirit and the revealed truth of God. Satan and his helpers do not fight mere religiosity; their foremost goal is to turn us away from God's truth.

When spiritualists (spiritists) claim that spiritism has strengthened their belief in life after death and deepened their religious devotion, this is to be granted. Religious ardor, even when it is sacrificial and high minded, is not the same as salvation through Christ and sanctification through the Holy Spirit and the Word of God.[34]

Spiritism and Christianity are poles apart and deadly enemies. One represents darkness, the other light. One denies every cardinal truth of God's Word, the other accepts all revealed truth. One is in complete rebellion to God, the other submits to God. Deliverance from the bondage of spiritism is possible only through Christ.[35] This is why psychiatry, psychology, and medical treatment are not sufficient for the healing of the whole man. Only the gospel of Christ and the liberating power of the Word of God can fully heal body, soul, and spirit.

NOTES
CHAPTER 3

1. Rudolf Tischner, *Ergebnisse Okkulter Forschung,* p. 167. Cf. Robert H. Thouless, "Spiritualism," *Encyclopaedia Britannica,* 21 (1964): 240-242; J. B. Rhine, "Spiritualism," *Encyclopedia Americana,* 25 (1951): 421-423; F. W. H. Myers, *Human Personality and Its Survival of Bodily Death,* 2 vols.
2. Kurt E. Koch, *Between Christ and Satan,* p. 124. The religions of the ancient Sumerians, Egyptians, Babylonians, Hittites, Assyrians, Chinese, Persians, Greeks, and Romans swarm with demons, that is, evil spirits who are the dynamic behind the idols and the gods of paganism (cf. T. Witton Davies, *Magic, Divination, and Demonology Among the Hebrews and Their Neighbors,* especially pp. 64-71). See also E. F. Hanson, *Demonology or Spiritualism, Ancient and Modern.*
3. Koch, *Between Christ and Satan,* pp. 123, 124; Koch, *Christian Counseling and Occultism,* pp. 28-41, 136-153. Cf. John L. Nevius'

study of "Spiritualism" in *Demon Possession,* 8th ed., pp. 314-332; Merrill F. Unger, *Biblical Demonology,* 8th ed., pp. 143-164; W. M'Donald, *Spiritualism Identical with Ancient Sorcery, New Testament Demonology and Modern Witchcraft;* A. Conan Doyle, *History of Spiritualism;* K. H. Porter, *Through A Glass Darkly.* For a brilliant and firsthand exposé of spiritualism (spiritism) by a spiritistic medium later converted to Christ, see Raphael Gasson, *The Challenging Counterfeit,* pp. 1-92.

4. Koch, *Between Christ and Satan,* p. 137; Hobart E. Freeman, *Deliverance from Occult Oppression and Subjection,* p. 38.

5. Nevius, p. 322.

6. Koch, *Between Christ and Satan,* p. 138. Powerful mediums are able to transfer coins and other objects from one locked or sealed container to another or cause such objects to vanish. Cf. Thouless, p. 241.

7. For example, Gullat-Wellenburg, *Der physikalische Mediumismus* (Berlin: Ullstein-Verlag, 1925), Table 3, Photo 13, p. 288.

8. Enno Nielsen, ed., *Das Grosse Geheimnis* (Ebenhausen near Munich, 1923), p. 216; Georg Homsten, *Okkultismus* (Berlin-Duesseldorf, 1950), p. 241. As an illustration of an interesting variety of telekinetic phenomena that took place in the flat in Cambridge, England, which became "haunted" after the death of the late Bishop James A. Pike's son, see James A. Pike and Diane Kennedy, *The Other Side* (New York: Dell Publishing Co., 1969), pp. 72-95; Hans Holzer, *The Psychic World of Bishop Pike,* pp. 89-128.

9. Koch, *Between Christ and Satan,* p. 125.

10. *Ibid.,* pp. 126, 127.

11. Diane Kennedy Pike, *Search,* pp. 124-130.

12. Swedenborg maintains "that his spiritual senses were opened so that he might be in the spiritual world as consciously as in this world. . . . Because of his other-world experiences, Swedenborg has been regarded as a spiritualistic 'medium' yet it may be observed that the normal idea of mediumship is reversed, the man being admitted into the spiritual world, not the spirits into the material world" (*Encyclopaedia Britannica,* 21 (1964): 653).

13. Koch, pp. 130, 131. For a remarkable case of protracted communication with the spirit world by means of automatic writing see Albert Payson Terhune and Anice Terhune, *Across the Line.* Anice Terhune allegedly communicated with her deceased husband, the well-known author of canine stories, via this method.

14. Cf. Tischner, pp. 42, 43.

15. Cf. Tischner, p. 41.

16. Cf. Koch, pp. 131, 132; James M. Gray, *Spiritism and the Fallen Angels,* pp. 17, 18, 21; William C. Irvine, *Heresies Exposed,* 11th ed., p. 175.

17. Such forms have been represented by flash camera in Baron Schrenck-Notzing's exhaustive work *Matérialisationphänomene,* a contribution to the mediumistic teleplastics (Munich: Reinhardt, 1914), plates 23-30, p. 237. The phenomena of materialization are also treated in the work of the French writer, Madame Bisson,

Les Phénomenès dits de matérialisation (Paris, 12th ed., 1921). Cf. also Gasson, pp. 80-84.

18. Besides the photographs in Schrenck-Notzing's work, actual paraffin molds are reported by *Zeitschrift für Arbeit und Besinnung* (Stuttgart: Quell Verlag, January 1, 1951), p. 19.

19. Walter Schäble, *Der grosse Zauber* (Gladbeck, Schriftenmissionsverlag, Gladbeck, 1950), p. 29; Tischner, p. 156.

20. Martensen Larsen, *Das Blendwerk des Spiritismus und die Rätsel der Seele* (Agentur des Rauhen Hauses, 1924), p. 37.

21. Koch, *Between Christ and Satan*, pp. 132-134.

22. Larsen, p. 20.

23. Cf. Nielsen, p. 141.

24. Koch, *Christian Counseling*, pp. 30, 31.

25. Koch, *Between Christ and Satan*, pp. 134-136. For a history of clairvoyant phenomena and divinatory prognostication see Arturo Castiglioni, *Adventures of the Mind*. For a study of extrasensory travel with alleged true case histories of people who have actually traveled outside their bodies, see Susy Smith, *The Enigma of Out-of-Body Travel*, pp. 9-146.

26. Cf. Koch, *Christian Counseling*, p. 29. Illustrations of this sort are abundantly attested by the materializations of the great mediums. Cf. Schrenck-Notzing, ed., *The Physical Phenomena of the Great Mediums*, pp. 100, 252.

27. Jung-Stilling, *Theorie der Geisterkunde* (Nurnberg: Zeitbuchverlag, 1921), 2: 101.

28. Koch, *Christian Counseling*, pp. 150, 151. Bishop Pike's now-famous "haunted" flat in Cambridge, England, has dramatized this phenomenon to an amazed world in Pike and Kennedy, pp. 72-95; Holzer, pp. 89-128.

29. Koch, *Between Christ and Satan*, pp. 30, 31. Cf. Rollo Ahmed, *The Black Art;* Gerald B. Gardner, *Witchcraft Today;* Montague Sommers, *The History of Witchcraft;* C. H. Wallace, *Witchcraft in the World Today*.

30. Quoted by Koch, p. 153. See Hans Bender, *Psychische Automatismen* (Leipzig: Freiburg, Verlag-Barth, 1936), *Zum Problem der ausserinlichen Wahrnehmung* (Leipzig: Verlag-Barth, 1936). Cf. Gasson, pp. 31-35.

31. For a full exposition of this incident see Unger, *Biblical Demonology*, 8th ed., pp. 148-152. Cf. Jules Michelet, *Satanism and Witchcraft;* William Seabrook, *Witchcraft*.

32. For an exhaustive study of counseling in the field of occultism see Koch, *Christian Counseling*, pp. 28-162.

33. *Ibid.,* pp. 153, 162.

34. For a more complete exposition of this fact, see chapter 8.

35. For a brief but comprehensive indictment of spiritism see Irvine, *Heresies Exposed*, pp. 174-180.

CHAPTER 4

Demons and Foretelling the Future

Fortune-telling is the art of forecasting future events and reading human character. Under the form of divination ("the faculty of foreseeing"; Latin, *divinare* "to foresee") it goes back to antiquity. Fortune-telling or divination was usually demon inspired (1 Corinthians 10:20). The word "divine" is derived from the Latin *divinus,* meaning "divinely inspired and pertaining to a deity (*divus*)." Thus a diviner is one who practices divination. He professes to predict future events or to reveal occult things by supernatural means.

Fortune-telling, or divination, is the offspring of idolatry. To seek intimate knowledge of the future is to impugn God's holy character. It is forbidden by his Word. Divination is a specialized form of magic. In magic, demonic agencies are resorted to for performing superhuman feats. In divination, magic is used in an attempt to foresee the future.

Divination relates to magic as prophecy relates to miracle. Both divination and prophecy imply special knowledge. In divination it is demonic; in prophecy it is godly. Magic is Satan's imitation of God's miracles. Divination is the satanic counterfeit of biblical prophecy.

Genuine fortune-telling or divination assumes the existence of superhuman spiritual beings. It also assumes that these beings possess knowledge which man does not have and that they are willing, upon certain conditions that are familiar to diviners, to transmit this information to man. Even Cicero in his famous treatise "Concerning Divination," although denying any superhuman communication on the part of the diviner, yet heartily endorsed a definition of divination as "a power in

55

man which foresees and explains those signs which the gods throw in his path."[1] Unless the demonic underlies the phenomena of fortune-telling at least indirectly, the practices in question are only clever trickery and excluded from the scope of this work.

Various forms of fortune-telling

The art of divination can be divided into two main categories. First is artificial or augural divination, when the fortune-teller interprets certain signs or omens under indirect demonic control. Second is inspirational divination, in which the medium is completely under the influence of demonic powers who enable him to foresee the future and utter oracles embodying what he sees, as in spiritism.

In ancient times, the conviction prevailed widely that not only oracles but omens of all types were given to men by "the gods" (demon powers). In the cases of supernatural intervention, the various forms of fortune-telling were real divinatory phenomena. Otherwise they were strictly in the category of hocus-pocus and swindle.

Astrology

Definition of astrology. Astrology is an ancient art or pseudoscience "which claims to forecast events on earth by observation of the fixed stars and of the sun, moon and planets."[2] Astrology also claims the ability to predict human character and fate. This is done through horoscopes which are based on the configuration of the heavens at the person's moment of birth. The point where the sun's path intersects the eastern horizon at the precise time of birth is noted. A chart of the heavens is then completed in which the positions of the heavenly bodies are studied. Their influence on the newborn child is deduced from the mythological character of the celestial orbs. This influence is modified by the positions and geometrical relationship between the planets, and the significance interpreted by astrologers.

The sun, moon, and planets in antiquity were considered as living beings ("gods," actually demons). As deities they were thought of as possessing preferred abodes or "houses" among the stars. An early astrological system divided the zodiac (the broad belt of constellations which the earth traverses during its annual trip around the sun) into twelve such houses. These were ingeniously assigned to the seven competing tenants (sun, moon, and five planets, the other planets not yet having been discovered). The assumption was that the sun, which gives light by day, and the moon, by night, needed only one house each. On the other hand the other five (?) planets needed two houses each, one for use by day, the other for use by night.

Another astrological arrangement of the twelve houses was devised by means of a geometrical construction, commencing from the point of intersection of the sun's ecliptic and the earth's horizon. This system included the whole sphere of the fixed stars and was not confined to the zodiac belt. To these houses, however determined, were allocated the various spheres of human life. The planets of the different houses were regarded as giving information about the matter pertaining to their supposed sphere of influence, such as life, death, wealth, marriage, children, friendships, enmities, and "fate" in general.[3] Professional astrologers work out horoscopes in varying degrees of detail.

Astrology and demonic deception. As a type of pagan divination, astrology invites the activity of demon spirits because it originated in star worship and seeks secret knowledge in opposition to God's will and God's Word. When an Israelite became implicated in star worship, sentence of death by stoning was pronounced upon him, emphasizing the flagrant violation of the first commandment such apostasy entailed (Deuteronomy 17:1-5; Exodus 20:1-5). Since astrology originated in idolatry, it invited the interference of demonic powers of the air (Ephesians 2:2), who seek to draw men away from the adoration of the one true God.

Star worship spread from Babylon to the nations that surrounded ancient Israel. Isaiah scornfully denounced it, deriding the Babylonian astrologers: "You are wearied with your many counsels; let them stand forth and save you, those who divide the heavens, who gaze at the stars, who at the new moon predict what shall befall you" (Isaiah 47:13, Hebrew). Jeremiah admonished the people not to be dismayed by the "signs of the heavens; because the heathen are dismayed at them!" (Jeremiah 10:2; cf. Daniel 2:27; 4:7).

As astrology spread to Greece, Rome, and later to Europe, it lost much of its religious character. Today we are witnessing a widespread revival of astrology.[4] People like to read about themselves and readily become avid horoscope readers. In some extreme cases of horoscope bondage, strange and tragic things happen. Dr. Koch tells of a woman who entered a police station and confessed that she had shot and killed her son. She did this because an astrologer predicted that the ill son would never regain normal mental health. To save her son from this horrible future, she killed him. The woman was arrested and sentenced after a prolonged trial, but the astrologer went free.[5]

Another example of a person under demonic compulsion to carry out an astrological prediction is found in the bizarre case of a young merchant. He had a detailed horoscope made which indicated that in the course of his life he would change his vocation three times. Accordingly, the young man began to attend night school and then to study for the Protestant ministry. Duly ordained, he was a Protestant clergyman for only a few years, when he was converted to Catholicism and became a Catholic priest. He still is driven by the overpowering compulsion that a third change in occupation is his inevitable "fate."[6]

Many who consider astrology as superstition and fraud have nevertheless come under its occult power by dabbling in it, either as a pastime or to expose its fraudulent character. A case in point is a minister who paid an expensive fee to have a detailed horoscope cast for himself with the avowed purpose of proving that astrology was nothing but ignorant superstition and a colossal fraud. So he confidently waited, assured that the horoscope would not fulfill its predictions. However, he was astonished to see the prophecies coming true, even to the smallest details.

As the years went by the minister grew uneasy and tried to figure out some rational explanation for this puzzle. He had the preconceived notion that astrological lore was only based on suggestion and superstition. It was utterly inconceivable that he as a Christian could be victimized by suggestion. Finally he concluded he had sinned through this experiment and had become the victim of evil spiritual powers working through the horoscope. He immediately repented and renounced all connection with astrology. To his surprise he now observed that his horoscope was no longer correct. It was a plain demonstration that demonic agencies are active in astrology. He knew that a person exposes himself to occult bondage and enslavement by complicity in spiritism. He now found the same to be true of astrology.[7]

Astrology as a fortune-telling art carries with it an occult tendency with all the effects of complicity in occultism in general. People who become dependent on the horoscope often develop psychic disturbances, such as fatalistic fear of life and a paralyzing melancholia. It discourages faith in God and a sense of his will and paralyzes initiative and power of judgment. Disorder and despair assume control of life. Every evidence of demonic influence in the personality becomes visible.

Astrology and satanic fraud. A Christian counselor should be cognizant of the problems involved in horoscope obsession. Simple fraud, overpowering suggestion, and demonism could be involved, and an understanding of their interrelation is necessary to deal with the occult effects they produce. It has already been shown how strong suggestion created by horoscope reading can result in demonic control of life, working out the astrological prediction. Only repentance toward God will break the occult connection and destroy the fatalistic compulsion to fulfill the horoscope prediction. The victim will then be free to make his own choice in the will of God. The counselor must point out that the only way to escape the snare of demonic influence is to avoid all complicity in astrological art.

The remaining problem of satanic fraud is of such colossal proportions that the whole traffic in horoscopy bears the clear impress of Satan, the liar and deceiver (cf. John 8:44). The modern form of astrology, though not following the naïve idolatry of the ancients, is just as blind to the operation of the same demonic powers. Current astrology sets aside God's Word and seeks knowledge of the future just as the Babylonian and Egyptian astrologers did. Complicity in astrology, whether innocent or informed, exposes one to occult influence.

From a scientific viewpoint as well as the spiritual, astrology deceives its devotees. Although it has changed its ancient costume, it still follows the old rules which are at variance with scientific astronomy. There is no convincing evidence even in the social sciences that planetary movements affect human actions, and the empirical science of astronomy flatly repudiates the mythology of astrology.

Astrology and moral decline. The upsurge in astrological interest[8] is unmistakable evidence of moral and social decay.[9] Occultism rises ominously in times of world turmoil, religious apostasy, and moral decline. Roman history illustrates this. Cicero and Cato vigorously opposed astrology in an era of robust cultural expression, but when later emperors employed astrologers, signs of decadence proliferated in the empire. Such signs are multiplying in the United States and throughout the world today.

Carroll Righter is the best known and most successful of U.S. astrologers. Dubbed "the dean of America's public astrologers,"[10] he is one of about 10,000 full-time and 175,000 part-time practitioners in the U.S. alone. Astrology is booming and like almost everything else is being computerized. A company called Time Pattern Research Institute, Inc., has programmed a computer to turn out a 10,000-word horoscope reading in two minutes. It set an early goal of 10,000 capacity in a month, with plans for continued expansion.

The commericial world, and especially show business and Wall Street, are dabbling in astrology. Seeress Sybil Leek's *Diary of a Witch* is a rapid seller and her alleged witchcraft seems mainly a device to distinguish her from such colleagues as Maurice Woodruff, who has done his foretelling on a syndicated TV show in a national women's magazine.

Immorality and purient tastes in literature, art, and music evidence the nation's spiritual ignorance and gullibility which foster frauds such as astrology. A healthy culture would not welcome and increasingly demand guidance from the stars for personal problems and momentous decisions. The intellectual sickness of our culture is confirmed by the deluge of astrological literature submerging faith in a personal God.

The inanity of horoscopes was demonstrated indirectly by the editor of a large daily newspaper who was forced to publish an outdated version when the new material failed to arrive in time for publication. Not one of the 100,000 readership complained of any irrelevance, so the editor concluded he could spare himself the cost of new horoscopes and reprint old ones. For three months he used outdated reprints, and then a reader complained that the sign of the zodiac did not check with the month. His reputation — and income — in jeopardy, the editor renewed his order for fresh material and restored his "trustworthy" horoscopes![11]

Card-laying

Definition of cartomancy. Cartomancy is the art of forecasting the future by the manipulation and placing of cards. The technique is simple since certain meanings are attached to certain cards. For instance, seven of hearts is a card of love, ten of hearts a fulfilled wish, while ten of spades is a lucky card. Thousands of combinations are possible with a pack of fifty-two playing cards.

Illustrations of card laying. This art is widely practiced. Although the gift of the well-known seeress Jeane Dixon operates in various ways, she sometimes uses a deck of cards to help see into the future. Ruth Montgomery, in the best seller *A Gift of Prophecy*[12] says that the famous clairvoyant sometimes uses a worn deck of cards. After requesting the subject to shuffle and cut, she holds them in her own hands but does not look at the faces of the cards. Nor do the cards even form a complete deck.

The seeress treasures them because a "sweet old gypsy" gave them to her when she was eight years old, and, "Because she blessed them, they carry good vibrations. I don't know a single thing about telling fortunes with cards. I simply have a person hold them so that I can pick up his vibrations. It sometimes helps me to pull out his channels," declares the seeress. She adds, "I keep that wornout old deck carefully wrapped in a handkerchief, because I just loved that gypsy."

In January 1948, Mrs. Dixon declared that Harry Truman would be reelected to a second term. She envisioned "Mr Dewey disappearing in a flood of newspapers . . . and a laurel wreath of victory descending over Mr. Truman's head." The prediction appeared so wild that the seeress tried to test it with a deck of cards. A witness said, "She brought out those old, worn cards that she sometimes uses, and had me cut them. Then she spread them out. She didn't say anything for a few minutes, but she finally looked up and said that she just couldn't see it any other way. *Truman was going to win."* And win he did — to the astonishment of the entire nation.[13]

Fortune-telling by the use of cards can be traced through many centuries. The Romans possessed a system of little tablets with inscribed symbols. Later, in the eighth century, cards were used. The practice of predicting the future, even where mediumistic abilities are not evident, can scarcely be called harmless unless, of course, it is nothing more than a hoax to make easy money or an amusing pastime.

A sixteen-year-old girl, anxious to know how long she would have to wait for her longed-for suitor, went to a card-laying fortune-teller. By the power of telepathy rather than cartomancy, the fortune-teller told the girl that her brother had had a serious motorcycle accident a year ago, that her mother had heart trouble, and that she was having trouble with her father. She did not tell the girl of her telepathic gifts but let her believe that she could read all this in the cards. Having won her confidence, she then gave her information about the future. Believing the ambiguous statements and adjusting herself to them, she became victimized by a fulfilment compulsion and by strong suggestion that warped her outlook and action.[14]

Card-laying and spiritism. But mediumistic abilities are frequently present in card-laying, fortune-telling, and general prognostication. Divining demons can operate through the human agent (medium), enabling him to act, think, and speak in a manner that is extrasensory and superphysical. It is not a rare thing to have a fortune-teller confess that at the moment of clairvoyance, an alien spirit comes over her, enabling her to utter things which she herself did not know. At the time she feels as if she were controlled by an evil spirit, but afterward she returns to a completely normal state.

Paul's encounter with the mediumistic fortune-teller at Philippi demonstrates that not everything in fortune-telling is fraud and humbug. Real fortune-telling powers are demonic. The girl told the truth, receiving her knowledge from demons (Acts 16:16-18). Her commendation of Paul and Silas as "servants of the most high God, which shew unto us the way of salvation" (Acts 16:17), demonstrates the subtlety of Satan in gaining followers for later deception. Paul's keen gift of discerning of spirits (1 John 4:1, 2), resulted in liberating the girl from her divining spirit. The incident shows how Satan frequently parades as an angel of light, especially under the guise of alleged religiosity.

The same problem presents itself with Jeane Dixon. Is she a bona-fide prophetess of God or a psychic medium for Satan? As to Mrs. Dixon herself, she is said to be a religious person who attends mass daily, says many prayers and does many good deeds. Because of her piety and her ability to predict future events, some claim that her gift is none other than the gift of prophecy mentioned by the Apostle Paul in 1 Corinthians 12:10.

A careful reading of the Word of God discredits this claim. In the first place, the Apostle Paul teaches that the gift of direct prophecy by the Holy Spirit (1 Corinthians 12:10) was to be temporary (13:8). The completion of the New Testament Scriptures would supersede the need for direct inspirational prophecy. Now that God's people have the completed Scriptures, we have all that God intended us to know about the future within the prophetic Scriptures. This at once makes Jeane Dixon's prophetic gift suspect.

Jeane Dixon cannot be classified as a genuine prophetess of the Lord despite the remarkable nature of her predictions. Her gift did not come through reading the Bible or a confrontation with God, but through a mysterious, fortune-telling gypsy she met when she was a girl of eight. This gypsy reputedly saw Jeane's potential powers of prophecy in the palm of her hand and gave her a crystal ball and a "blessed" deck of cards to use in her career.

There is a third reason why Jeane Dixon cannot be accepted as a genuine prophetess of the Lord. The expressions of her gift are as questionable as its beginnings. She uses occult methods common to pagan divination and psychic mediumship. As a girl, she began to see "pictures" in the crystal ball the gypsy gave her, and soon was able to read people's fortunes and to forecast events. She also writes horoscopes for numerous newspapers.

Mrs. Dixon has predicted many things of worldwide significance, such as the sudden death of President Franklin Roosevelt, the partitioning of India, the Communist takeover of China, the rise and fall of Nikita Khruschev, the orbiting of Sputnik by the Russians, the assassination of President John F. Kennedy, etc. Nevertheless, her predictions often descend to trivial and worldly levels. She is able to predict the success or failure of theatrical plays, the outcome of a horse race, or the danger of "unlucky" garments. Common sense tells us that the Holy Spirit of God has nothing to do with such mundane predictions. God does not bestow his gifts for vain reasons.

The conclusion seems inescapable. Jeane Dixon is to be classified as a psychic medium, though of very superior qualities. Possessing great sensitivity to spirits that are "not of God" (1 John 4:1), she does not need to go into a trance, as does the average medium. These spirits are indeed demons. It must be remembered that not all demons are vile, threatening, or openly "bad." Spirits may appear religious, refined, and "good" in a qualified sense. Their distinguishing trait is that they are *"not* of God" — they are opposed to God's Word and God's will and to the Person and work of our Lord. This stamps them as "demon spirits" (1 John 4:2) and differentiates them from the pure, unfallen angels and from the Holy Spirit.

Psychometry

Definition: Psychometry is a type of clairvoyance that can identify the characteristics of an individual through some object he wore or used. Some parapsychologists try to explain this phenomenon by assuming that clothing and objects used daily become impregnated by the owner. The psychometric clairvoyant is assumed to be able to lay hold of and to interpret mental-psychic impressions that have emanated from the person in question to objects he wore or used.

Occultism and psychometry. The true explanation of psychometric phenomena lies in mediumistic fortune-telling, not in pseudoscientific parapsychology. This conclusion is confirmed when Christian counseling with cases of psychometry reveals occult bondage. A young man with remarkable psychometric powers could identify an unknown person by a few handwritten lines. By concentrating on the handwriting the lad could give exact statements concerning the person's address, family background, health, etc. When he expressed a desire to admit Christ into his life, an inward resistance became so tremendous that he fainted during prayer. It turned out that he was relying on a dangerous magic book which has circulated in occult circles in Europe for centuries, called *The Sixth and Seventh Books of Moses*.[15] This association clearly points to the demonic character of psychometry and its close alliance with black magic.

Palmistry

Definition: Palmistry is fortune-telling through the inter-preting of the lines in a person's palm. Palmistry can be traced back to ancient Rome. Astrological concepts were in-troduced into palmistry. The palm of the hand is divided into four main lines (heart, head, fate, and life) and into seven planet mounds. Below the thumb is the Venus mound, and from the index finger to the little finger are Mercury, Apollo, Saturn, and Jupiter Mounds, with the Mars and Moon Mounds located under the little finger.

Palmistry, like card-laying, astrology, and other forms of fortune-telling, can stimulate a strong compulsion in the indi-vidual to fulfill the predictions of the fortune-teller. If the fortune-teller is a spiritistic medium, psychic bondage to de-mons may result, as in all occult practice. Fortune-telling, in any case, can produce harmful effects and may lead to disas-ter.

Divining rod and pendulum

Common method of divination. "The wide use of the ex-ploratory pendulum in Western Europe, in what has come to be called 'radiesthesia,' is essentially similar to the method of the divining rod."[16] The turning of the rod (hazel twig) or the swinging of the pendulum, which supposedly indicates the location of the hidden object in question, can undoubtedly be accounted for sometimes by "unconscious muscular move-ment," as parapsychologist J. B. Rhine contends, but "if there is reliable knowledge obtained by either the divining rod or the pendulum that could not have come from sensory percep-tion or inferences, we should presumably have to turn for an explanation to clairvoyance, precognition, or some form of ex-trasensory perception."[17]

Professor Rhine is dealing in the extraordinary phenomena that undulate between the natural and the supernatural, the physical and the superphysical, but as a scientist he discounts any theory that postulates evil supernaturalism. To be fully meaningful, the scientific studies in parapsychology that he has conducted with such distinction at Duke University since 1934 must take into consideration the reality of the spirit world of evil (Satan and demons).[18]

To limit the scientific to the natural plane of existence is to omit some of the data responsible for certain natural effects. The result of such study is a tendency to explain away rather than objectively explain supernatural events and to end up with learned theories that ignore part of the evidence. This is where current parapsychological studies stand. They are, however, exceedingly valuable in focusing scientific interest on the supernatural realities behind occultism. They could advance to great achievements if they would recognize the influence of evil supernaturalism in psychic activities.

Phenomena of rod and pendulum practice. A dowser attempts to locate underground water, minerals, or oil by using a forked twig as a divining rod. When the dowser grasps the rod and walks about, the twig is supposed to dip to indicate water, minerals, or oil directly below. The practice is very ancient and is still widely followed in Europe, Africa, Australia, and America. Sir William Barrett, a physicist, declared flatly that the successful dowser has clairvoyant powers by which he is subconsciously guided.[19]

Through the rod and pendulum, the occult practitioner can also describe and locate persons through objects from their bodies, as a handkerchief or tie, or by means of a photograph. Lost objects can be found, criminals traced, disease diagnosed, medicines prescribed, or physical healing by psychic power effected, etc.[20] In practically all of these cases, some form of occult oppression can develop in both those who practice the art and those who seek its help. Where mediumistic gifts are lacking, such methods of foretelling the future or finding occult information are largely if not entirely a clever hoax.

Prophetic dreams and visions

Distinction in terminology. A dream represents the fanciful thoughts of a person while he is asleep, but it has been used by God to guide someone under special circumstances or in some unusual crisis (cf. Matthew 1:20; 2:13; Acts 2:17).[21] A vision usually occurs in a state of emotional ecstasy or a trance when the subject is awake. Prognostic dreams and visions are those that have a prophetic cast and reveal the future.

In biblical times God's servants had visions and dreams under special circumstances, as in the case of Jacob's ladder vision at Bethel (Genesis 28:11-15) when he was fleeing from Esau's rage and leaving the land of Canaan. Isaiah had a vision of the Lord's glory (Isaiah 6:1-11). John had a vision also when he was inspired to receive the prophetic revelation that was to be the capstone of the New Testament. But the gift of direct, inspirational prophecy ended when the Scriptures were completed, according to 1 Corinthians 13:8-10. No further revelations of future events are intimated or authenticated by Scripture, so we should carefully "test the spirits" that offer knowledge of the future (1 John 4:1, 2).

Demonism and current prophetic visions. The remarkable visions of Jeane Dixon, the most famous seeress of the century, call for evaluation. In her first vision, on July 14, 1952, she saw a huge serpent twisting by the side of her bed and then slowly entwining itself around her body. She says, "While I watched, it slowly turned its eyes and gazed into mine. . . . The steady gaze of the reptile was permeated with love, goodness, strength, and knowledge. A sense of 'peace on earth, good will toward men' coursed through my being."[22] Amazingly, Mrs. Dixon considers this first vision the key to the others. In Scripture the serpent is a symbol of evil (Genesis 3:1; Revelation 12:9-12; 20:1-3), and its appearance in this key vision suggests that deceptive spirits are indeed the source of her revelations (1 Timothy 4:1; 1 John 4:1, 2).

Mrs. Dixon had her second vision while she was praying and meditating in St. Matthew's Cathedral in Washington. She was about to burn candles when "a mass of purple and gold balls . . . floated upward and . . . encircled the knees of the statue of the Virgin Mary, rising gently . . . enveloped her breast and head, like an uptilted halo." The rest of the cathedral vision caused her to declare: "A remarkable peace overcame me and I knew that a council of our church would soon bring together under the roof of the Holy See in Rome the religions and nationalities of all the world." Four years later the Roman Catholic Church began the fulfillment of her vision in the Ecumenical Council of 1962 (cf. Revelation 17: 1-8).[23]

In her third vision, the seeress saw the papal throne vacant and the papacy suffering violence, a prophecy clearly outlined in Revelation 17:15-18, when the political power of the end time destroys the ecclesiastical power headed up by Rome. The fourth vision, which the seeress believes to be the most important of all, was received February 5, 1962, when a rare conjunction of the planets took place and astrologers were forecasting some great event.

At this time strange happenings began to occur in Mrs. Dixon's home. Lights began to dim and flare. As she gazed toward the East before sunrise she saw an Egyptian Pharaoh and Queen Nefertiti stepping out of the sun's rays. Cradled in the queen's arm was a baby in rags, in stark contrast to the gorgeous robes of the royal couple.

While the seeress gazed entranced, the couple advanced toward her and extended the baby, whose eyes were full of wisdom, as if offering it to the entire world. Soon the baby grew and became a man before Mrs. Dixon's eyes. A small cross which had formed above him began to grow in size until it extended over the earth. Then people of every race were seen kneeling and adoring this man. Her interpretation was: "A child, born somewhere in the Middle East shortly after 7 A.M. (EST) on February 5, 1962, will revolutionize the world. Before the close of the century he will bring together all mankind in one all-embracing faith. This will be the foundation of a new Christianity, with every sect and creed united through this man who will walk among the people to spread the wisdom of the Almighty Power."[24]

Bible-taught Christians immediately recognize the characteristics of the *Antichrist*, not an ambassador of God, in this vision. Prophecy-minded Christians are appalled to read of this seeress joining in the adoring worship of the "child of the East." She declares: "I felt like a tiny seed ready to sprout and grow, but I was only one of millions of similar seeds. I knew within my heart, 'Here is the beginning of wisdom.' "

By the time her second book was published in 1969, Mrs. Dixon had reversed her interpretation of the "child of the East," without acknowledging her earlier gross error. In *My Life and Prophecies* she radically changes the meaning of her visions while scarcely changing their details by recalling:

"Suffering people, of all races, knelt in worshipful adoration, lifting their arms and offering their hearts to the man. For a fleeting moment I felt as though I were one of them, but the channel that emanated from him was not that of the Holy Trinity . . . here was something God allowed me to see without my becoming a part of it. . . . There is no doubt in my mind that the 'child' is the actual person of the Antichrist, the one who will deceive the world in Satan's name."[25]

Also in her second book Mrs. Dixon reevaluates the significance of the serpent who appeared in her first — and key — vision. She quotes some Scripture about the "dragon" and the devil and concludes:

"The first and most important part of my vision of the serpent was clarified. There was no doubt that the scholars were right when they asserted that 'the serpent among Christians is nothing else than the symbol of Satan, whose head will be crushed by the Son of Man when he comes.' For the Christian, the serpent, the dragon of the Bible, is linked directly with the figure of the Antichrist (a man, a 'prince of peace,' who will appear on the world scene claiming to be Christ), who will be one of the several signs of the second coming of Christ."[26]

Obviously, Mrs. Dixon knew her Bible better when she wrote her second book than when she produced her first! But what was the *source* of her visions? The Bible tells us they were *not* from God, because his prophets speak the *truth* (Deuteronomy 18:21, 22). The only other source of secret knowledge is *Satan*. And when satanic messages use the words and scenes of Scripture, the guidance is treacherous indeed! (Luke 4:1-13)

Moreover, God's Word warns against extra-biblical prophecies and revelations. All that the Christian needs to know concerning the future is revealed in the prophetic Scriptures. Direct inspirational prophecies and knowledge in addition to the Word of God are not now needed and are not now given by the Spirit of God (1 Corinthians 13:8, 9).

Since the completed written Word, called in Greek *to teleiton,* "the completed (final) thing" (1 Corinthians 13:10), has been recorded in the canonical Scriptures of the New Testament, the Spirit reveals what has been written. What pretends to be revealed apart from what has been written is to be accounted suspect by all who honor the written Word of God.

How to evaluate fortune-telling

Biblical verdict. Because all forms of fortune-telling promote superstition and idolatry, divination of any sort is condemned and rigidly banned for God's people by the Word of God. Spiritistic fortune-tellers and clairvoyants were subject to the death penalty in Israel (Leviticus 19:31; 20:6, 27). Anyone who used "divination" or was "an observer of times, or an enchanter, or a witch (fortune-teller), or a (magic) charmer, or a consulter with familiar spirits (a medium), or a wizard (clairvoyant), or a necromancer (one who communicated with the spirit-world)" was outlawed from the community of the Lord's people (Deuteronomy 18:10, 11). The same stringent prohibition runs throughout Scripture (cf. 1 Chronicles 10:13; Isaiah 8:19; 44:25; Ezekiel 21:26; Micah 3:6, 7; Jeremiah 29:8; Zechariah 10:2). The New Testament takes the same firm stand (Acts 16:16-18; Galatians 5:20).

Risk of involvement. Whoever resorts to fortune-telling in any form runs the risk of becoming occultly subjected and oppressed. Christian counseling has revealed disturbance to body, soul, and spirit among those who are engaged or connected with any type of divination. The irreligious person who engages in this forbidden art shows extreme callousness and resistance toward spiritual truths. The pious religionist who dab-

bles in the occult displays spiritual pride, self-righteous phari-
saism, opposition to pure doctrine of the Word, and a condition of insulation against the Holy Spirit.

Many weaknesses and vices often go hand in hand with
fortune-telling. A very high tendency to addictions (drugs,
tobacco, alcohol, sexual excesses) and to general immorality
are present. From the medical and psychiatric standpoint,
families bound by fortune-telling show a remarkably high in-
cidence of nervous disorders, mental illnesses, mediumistic psy-
choses, and many psychosomatic disorders.

NOTES

CHAPTER 4

1. Cicero, Marcus Tullius, *De Diviatione,* A. S. Pease, ed. (Urbana: University of Illinois, 1920), 2: 63.
2. Benjamin Farrington, "Astrology" in *Encyclopaedia Britannica,* 2 (1964): 640. For a standard work by a modern astrologer see A. J. Pearce, *The Text Book of Astrology,* 2nd ed. See also F. Ball and C. Bezold, *Sternglaube und Sterndeutung;* R. Eisler, *The Royal Art of Astrology;* Lynn Thorndike, *A History of Magic and Experimental Science,* vols. 1-4.
3. Farrington, p. 641, columns 1, 2. For a classic on ancient astrology see A. Bouche-Leclerg, *L'Astrologie grecque;* R. C. Thompson, ed. and trans., *The Reports of the Magicians and Astrologers at Nineveh and Babylon in the British Museum,* 2 vols.; O. Neugebauer, *The Exact Sciences in Antiquity;* F. Cumont, *Les Religions orientales dans le paganisme Romain,* 4th ed.
4. See *Time,* March 21, 1969, pp. 47-56. "Astrology columns now run in some 1,200 of the 1,750 dailies in the U. S." (p. 56). President Nixon's horoscope appears on p. 55, under 1969 predictions by Doris Kaye. "But there are many troubled people who refuse to accept personal responsibility for their lives, insisting that some outer force is in control. For these, a first-class astrologer can seem a necessity . . ." (p. 56).
5. Kurt E. Koch, *Between Christ and Satan,* pp. 13, 14.
6. Koch, pp. 20, 21.
7. *Ibid.,* pp. 21, 22. Cf. Charles S. Braden, "Astrology" in *The New Schaff-Herzog Religious Encyclopedia,* p. 91; Evangeline Adams, *Astrology for Everyone.*
8. "Astrology and the New Cult of the Occult," *Time,* March 21, 1969, pp. 47-56. There is great interest today "in witchcraft and tarot card reading. Occult book stores are booming," *Life,* 68, no. 1 (January 9, 1970); p. 17.
9. Cf. Hans Schwendimann, "Gegen die Not des Aberglaubens," Installment 3 in *Wahrsagerei und ihre Folgen* (St. Gallen: Kommis-

sionsverlag, Evangelische Buchhandlung), p. 15; A. Köberle, *Die Seele des Christentums* (Berlin, Furch-Verlag, 1932), pp. 81, 101.

10. "Astrology: Fad and Phenomenon" in *Time*, March 21, 1969, p. 47.
11. Koch, *Christian Counseling and Occultism*, p. 79.
12. Ruth Montgomery, *A Gift of Prophecy*, p. 26.
13. Gordon Lindsay, "Jeane Dixon — Prophetess or Psychic Medium?", pp. 7, 14.
14. Koch, *Between Christ and Satan*, p. 25.
15. This is the principal work on magic in Europe. Moses had nothing to do with its magic charms and formulas, which instruct in occultism, particularly how to establish rapport with Satan and demons. Its title is a deceptive pseudonym to trap the unwary.
16. J. B. Rhine, "Divination" in the *Encyclopedia Americana*, 9 (1951): 199. For a history of divination see Arturo Castiglioni, *Adventures of the Mind*. For a detailed study of the rod and pendulum in the mantic art see Koch, *Christian Counseling*, pp. 81-93.
17. Rhine, *loc. cit.*
18. Rhine et al., *Extra-Sensory Perception After Sixty Years;* J. B. Rhine and J. G. Pratt, *Parapsychology;* G. R. Price, "Science and the Supernatural," *Science,* 122 (August 26, 1955): 359-367; "The Controversy in Science over ESP," *Journal of Parapsychology,* 19 (1955): 236-271. See also the periodicals *Journal of Parapsychology: Proceedings of the Society for Psychical Research; Journal of the American Society for Psychical Research.*
19. William Barrett and Theodore Besterman, *The Divining Rod.* For a critical discussion of the divining rod see A. J. Ellis, *The Divining Rod, a History of Water Witching* (Washington D.C.: U. S. Geological Survey, 1917).
20. For examples of these phenomena in actual counseling experiences, see Koch, *Between Christ and Satan*, pp. 39-52; *Christian Counseling,* pp. 84, 85, 88, 91-93.
21. For a discussion of dreams recorded in Scripture see the author's *Biblical Demonology*, pp. 127-129.
22. Montgomery, p. 165.
23. Lindsay, p. 23.
24. Montgomery, p. 181.
25. Jeane Dixon, *My Life and Prophecies*, pp. 194, 203.
26. *Ibid.,* p. 174.

Demons and Magic

A s an ingredient of idol worship, magic goes back to antiquity. By virtue of their multiplicity and limited knowledge and power, the gods (demons) of paganism are incapable of establishing stability and security in society. "This deficiency forced both gods and men to make use of magic — an inactive power independent of gods and men, but which could be activized by the aid of incantations and rituals in order to accomplish supernatural deeds."[1]

Sumero-Akkadian and Canaanite religious literature amply attest the employment of magic by gods (i.e., demons) to accomplish definite purposes. The Babylonian Creation Epic (*Enuma Elish*) reports that in the struggle against the primeval pair, Tiamat and Apsu, the hero of the young generation of gods, Ea-Enki, killed Apsu with the aid of a spell which he recited.[2] It was by virtue of his knowledge of effective spells and rituals that Ea-Enki had the title "Lord of Incantation" and was reputed to be the god of magic par excellence.

In a battle with Tiamat, Marduk, the champion of the gods, used among other weapons a "red paste" which he held between his lips, red being the magic color for warding off evil influences.[3] Moreover, before proclaiming Marduk as their chief god, the gods in assembly tested him to ascertain whether he possessed the requisite knowledge of magic, without which no god could rule supreme. By his spoken word he made a piece of cloth vanish and reappear (be restored).[4]

Insight into the magical lore of the inhabitants of Canaan, and of the surrounding nations who became Israel's neighbors after the conquest, is furnished by the religious epics from

Ugarit and the Hebrew Scriptures. When Keret, king of Ugarit, fell ill, the supreme deity of the Ugaritic pantheon, El, healed him by magic.[5] The Hebrews were continually beset by the temptation to yield to the magical practices of their pagan neighbors, as amply attested by the Old Testament.[6]

The concept of magic

Scholars view magic from different perspectives. Both the naturalistic historian of religions and the scientist who rule out the supernatural reach different conclusions than the theologian and Christian counselor who take into account God's revelation concerning Satan and demons. Edwin Tylor, the great pioneer in anthropology, regarded magic as "an elaborate and systematic pseudo-science."[7] Sir James Frazer, the Scottish anthropologist, viewed it as "a spurious system of natural law as well as a fallacious guide of conduct; it is a false science as well as an abortive art."[8] All such definitions that leave out the insight of divine revelation cannot probe to the heart of the reality of magic.

An adequate definition of magic. Magic — like divination — is the divinely forbidden art of bringing about results beyond human power by recourse to superhuman spirit agencies (Satan and demons). In the widest sense of this definition, divination is but a species of magic employed as a means of securing secret and illegitimate knowledge, especially of the future. Divination is related to biblical prophecy as magic is related to divine miracle.

Divination calls forth special knowledge, but it is demonic. True prophecy also enlists special knowledge, but its source is divine. Magic brings special power into play, but its source is diabolic. On the other hand, the true miracle issues from God. As both magic and divination are rooted in demonic power, they are closely akin.

The word "magic" is derived from a Greek adjective (*magikē*), with the noun *technē* (art) implied. The full phrase, accordingly, is "magical art," occurring in the apocryphal book of the *Wisdom of Solomon* (17:7). But the noun "magic" stems from the *magi* or Zororastrian priests, demonstrating that magic historically is the art practiced in ancient Persia by the recognized priests of that country.[9]

Magic and extrasensory phenomena. Magic has been commonly defined as of two kinds: personal, and impersonal. Impersonal magic is little more than superstition when natural law is thought to be set aside or influenced by incantations, spells, amulets, charms, etc., apart from the intervention of spiritual beings. Even when the activities are thought to be solely impersonal, such is *not* the case if magical events occur.

If magic is genuine and not mere deception or hocus-pocus, it must be personal. Living, intelligent spirit beings become the real agents. Men, by incantations and ceremonies, actually influence and even control these spirit agents. The activity of such superphysical agents of evil produces the extrasensory phenomena of magic, that is, occurrences that transcend the normal operation of physical law and the perception of man's five senses.

Because of widespread denial of the reality of supernatural power — both divine and demonic, confusion abounds concerning the nature of magic. The psychiatrist, the medical doctor, the practicing occultist, the folklorist historian, and the liberal theologian will have a different view of magic than the serious student of the Bible.

Examples of extrasensory phenomena in the realm of magic are as impressive as such occurrences in the spheres of spiritism and fortune-telling.[10] Diseases, for example, can be magically diagnosed and cured. Just as the clairvoyant fortune-teller can identify the characteristics of an individual through some object from his person, so a lay medical practitioner who mixes magic with medicine can diagnose diseases and effect a cure.

Such a combination is practiced in Europe by the two Seiler brothers of Ottenheim, Baden, in their lay medical practice. By putting himself in a trance in his office, one of the brothers can identify all diseases of the patients in the waiting room and can afterward give a correct diagnosis in each case.[11] In Alsace, on the other hand, a Catholic priest nicknamed

"Pater Slipper" can diagnose diseases when the sick send him one of their slippers on which to concentrate.[12] In Germany, Switzerland, France, and other European countries, urine is also employed as a psychometrical means of contact with the ill, not for a laboratory analysis, but for clairvoyant diagnosis.

The history of magic is replete with extraordinary extrasensory phenomena that involve the spirit realm and every phase of the natural world as well, including human beings, animals, plants, and inorganic matter. Spirit-rapping, apparitions, ghosts, moving of furniture, and playing of musical instruments by invisible hands, stones falling from a ceiling, magical killing of cattle and blighting of crops, etc., are just a few of the weird occurrences that fill the annals of occult practice. "Incredible as it may seem," writes Hobart E. Freeman, "nevertheless even in this modern scientific age millions are now, or have been at some time, involved in some manner with ancient magic practices and rites, ranging from the charming of warts and burns to the use of spells, magic herbs, and hex signs on houses and barns (which can still be seen in some areas)."[13]

The character of magic

The precise character of magic has been even more heatedly disputed than its definition. One lauds it as a gift from God. Another denounces it as an operation of Satan and demons. Another denies it any moral quality and views it merely as the working of neutral forces of nature, which can be employed either positively or negatively. The liberal theologian sees it as the crystallization of time-bound ideas and customs. The psychologist looks at the magically subjected person as wrongly adjusted to life and the natural world. The psychiatrist sees the whole magical complex as symptomatic of mental aberration.

Magic and religion. That magic had no legitimate place in the true monotheistic faith of Israel nor in true spiritual Christianity is obvious from the nature of the phenomenon. In seeking to employ the power of Satan and demons to effect results contrary to God's will and in defiance of God's power, magic patently aligns itself against God and genuine religion.

Being in the nature of deception and mere superstition where it does not enlist the power of darkness, and possessing the character of diabolic miracle where it does, magic is opposed to and at complete variance with the revelation of God in Christ. Christianity can tolerate magic only as Christianity becomes corrupt. Magic can exist in the cults and perversions of Christianity, but not in unadulterated Christian faith.

Magic can — and does — flourish in non-Christian religions, where idolatry prevails and the moral laws of God are not followed. Its dynamic is demonism (1 Corinthians 10:20).

Biblical denunciation of magic. Since magic operates in the sphere of diabolic miracle and deception, the Bible condemns and forbids it. To the Hebrews, the pagan deities served by magicians were evil spirits. To deal in the occult was tantamount to acknowledging these deities and was an infraction of the first commandment of the decalogue (Exodus 20:1-6; Deuteronomy 18:9, 10).

Though Scripture condemns magic, it clearly recognizes the reality of its power. In the account of the Egyptian plagues (Exodus 7-11), it is taken for granted that the magicians of Egypt had power to perform supernatural feats (2 Timothy 3:8), as did the magicians in Babylon (Daniel 1:20; 2:2, 27; 4:7, 9; 5:11).

Human history will end with a tremendous demonic revival (Revelation 9:1-20) that will culminate in the reign of Antichrist, who will be attended by diabolic signs and magical wonders (2 Thessalonians 2:9-12; Revelation 13:13-18). Armageddon will be a demon-energized revolt against God and a satanic attempt to take over the earth (Revelation 16:13, 14).

The origin and aim of magic

Magic and the fall of man. Magic came into being with the spiritual fall of man at the threshold of human history. God's command to unfallen man was, "Fill the earth, and subdue it" (Genesis 1:28, Hebrew). The Creator thus ordered man to master earth's potentialities in dependence upon God and in the will of God. Satan, the author of confusion, offered man a knowledge and power contrary to God's will: "Ye shall be as God, knowing good and evil" (Genesis 3:5, Hebrew). The desire and drive for knowledge and power in opposition to the command and will of God constitutes the essence of magic. Facing this offer, young mankind found itself at the crossroads of destiny.

Magic and man's rebellion. Man listened to Satan's proposal and chose to disobey God. In his quest for knowledge and power, he became God's rival. God's display of wisdom and power was to be offset by man's display, as man came under Satan's dominion. Satan was to work through man to oppose God's plans for mankind and the earth.

Magic is another form of rebellion as man turned his allegiance from God and aligned himself with other gods (demons). He not only worshiped them but enlisted their help in his search for a knowledge and power that would enable him to live without God and in active opposition to him. The choice has always been the same: either man accepts God's salvation and submits to God's will, or he rebels and attempts to subdue the earth with the help of the devil.

In the light of divine revelation, it is futile to dispute the evil nature of magic. It is definitely immoral because it violates the moral law of God. To praise it as a gift of God displays ignorance of God's Word. To regard it as harmless is to ignore its spiritual — and physical — blight on its devotees.

The aim of magic. As a colossal revolt against God with the avowed satanic purpose of instilling in fallen man the desire to be "like the Most High" (Isaiah 14:14), magic seeks to deceive as many human beings as possible. To this end, demonic forces are engineering the gigantic apostasy of the end time that will culminate in the rise of Antichrist and the greatest demonstration of diabolic miracle and demonic wonders the world has ever seen (2 Thessalonians 2:8-10; Revelation 13:1-18). The demon-inspired campaign that issues in Armageddon represents Satan's attempt to take over the earth and banish the name of God and his Christ from this planet (Revelation 16:13, 14).

Christ's triumphant return will smash Satan's plan and result in the imprisonment of Satan and the demons in the abyss during the Millennium (Revelation 20:1-3; Zechariah 13:2). The temporary loosing of Satan at the end of the Millennium will prove the utter incorrigibility of this spirit-rebel and seal his doom in Gehenna (Revelation 20:10-15).

Endowment with magical powers

Proficiency in occultism in general combined with abilities and gifts in magical arts in particular is not an accident. Endowment with magical powers may be the result of a number of factors. First, and perhaps foremost, is heredity. Also important are occult transference, subscriptions to Satan, and occult experimentation.

Heredity and magical powers. Occult powers and magical abilities are passed on in hereditary succession, frequently through four generations. As an offshoot of idolatry, magic, like spiritistic mediumship, is an infraction of the first commandment of the divine moral law. It carries the following penalty: "I, the Lord thy God, am a jealous God, visiting the iniquity of the fathers upon the children unto the third and fourth generation of them that hate me" (Exodus 20:5). As the one true and only deity, God is "jealous" of idolatry because it is a flagrant affront to his holiness and incomparable character. Thus demonic worship invites the punishment of God to the third and fourth generations of those who despise God in this manner.

The general history of occultism shows that mediumistic powers can often be traced through four generations. It is a common thing for a dying father to bestow upon his eldest son or daughter his magical abilities. Sometimes the death of such magicians becomes a nightmare of suffering when children do not wish to receive the occult power. In anguish, the dying person complains that he cannot find "rest" till he finds someone to take over his magical powers. Sometimes distant relatives or an outsider will step in and receive the occult legacy.

Occult transference of magical powers. Sometimes magical powers are transferred by the occult ceremony of laying on of hands, a counterpart to the biblical custom (cf. Acts 8:17; 19:6; cf. Deuteronomy 34:9). The history of occult practice often relates how one or more magicians, particularly those adept in black (devil) magic, impart occult gifts of healing or clairvoyant and mediumistic abilities by placing their hands upon the head of a person desiring them and uttering magic charms and incantations.[14]

Subscription to Satan and magical powers. Magical powers may be acquired by signing an agreement with Satan, often in one's own blood. This is an age-old phenomenon. Isaiah mentions "making a covenant with hell" (28:15). Such blood-bound occultists frequently become endowed with astonishing magic capabilities. However, they become demonic captives and may be delivered only with the greatest difficulty. Often they become hopelessly shackled. As the redeemed Christian yields his body to God (Romans 12:1, 2), so the child of the devil may yield himself unreservedly to the powers of darkness. By this surrender he expects to attain occult abilities that God has forbidden or withheld.[15]

This practice of satanic blood pacts is not a mere superstitious hangover from medieval witchcraft and hobgoblins. It is a well-known and fairly common custom today in various rural districts of Europe where magic literature has circulated for centuries and magical powers have passed from one generation to another.

Occult experimentation and magical powers. Magical powers can also be acquired through dabbling in the occult. A factory worker in a Swiss town grew weary of his job and became enamored with tales of easy money made by occult healers and mesmerizers. He purchased some magic literature and started mastering charms and spells, underwent devils' ceremonies, and began healing experiments. His magic healing ability developed rapidly. He soon found his income far exceeded his former wages.[16]

The forms of magic

Numerous forms of magic exist. Among them are black magic, white magic, neutral magic, mental suggestion, criminal hypnosis, and magical mesmerism. When any of these forms enlist demonic powers, they are authentic cases of magic. In the absence of occult powers, the phenomena do not belong to the field of magic.

Black magic

Magic and medieval black arts. Magic has not changed since the Middle Ages. The term "black art" was then applied to magic because those proficient in it were considered to be in league with the powers of darkness.[17] The term "black magic" refers to the art of producing supernatural effects by direct league with Satan and demons. Frequently those who practice black magic make an actual pact with the powers of darkness, signing their allegiance to the devil in their own blood. This ceremony has come down from the Middle Ages to present-day Europe, where it is practiced in parts of Germany, France, and Switzerland. The ritual of signing an agreement involves a complete sell-out to the devil.

The practice of black magic. Some magic involves the direct solicitation and help of demons, specifically the devil.[18] It is the most terrible and powerful form of occult art, majoring in enchantment for persecution and vengeance, but also employing diabolical powers for defense and healing. An example of this nefarious practice is found in the death spells cast by witch doctors among aboriginal people, such as the Papuans on the island of New Guinea.

Enchantment for persecution and vengeance, as well as for defense and healing, is still practiced today, not only in pagan cultures but also in civilized lands where occultism flourishes. Literature on magic is still circulated, and its directives for incantations, charms, and spells are still followed in parts of Germany, France, and Switzerland.

A German farmer, who had never been troubled with psychic disturbances, returned home from a Russian prison camp and suddenly found himself suffering from acute fear-dreams. He had the feeling during sleep that a neighbor lady, the mother of his war comrade who was still missing in Russia, was strangling him. The tormented man went to an occultist who told him he was under magic persecution. The neighbor woman was seeking revenge on him for his good fortune in the light of her son's bad fortune. With the occultist's help, the terror-dreams ceased.

Then the ex-soldier found himself under a new attack: the neighbor was causing his cattle to die, head after head. The conjurer promised to remedy this new menace. Scraps of paper inscribed with magical formulae were to be mixed with the food of the cattle. The astonishing result was the cessation of the cattle epidemic.[19]

In addition to many cases of persecution and self-defense by black magic, occult healings are also common. One of the most striking came to light as a result of Dr. Kurt Koch's evangelistic and counseling ministry in Toggenburg, Switzerland. A local farmer came for counseling and related the tragic results of charming by black magic. As a boy, the farmer's son had become paralyzed after an attack of polio. The doctor was called too late, and the boy remained paralyzed. The farmer, desiring an able-bodied heir to take over the farm, tried everything possible. Finally he went to the notorious magician, Hugentobler in Peterzell. He healed the boy through black magic, so that the paralysis disappeared completely.

For several years everything went well. However, when the son was sixteen years old, his father found him in the stable with a cut artery in his neck. Tragedy had struck out of a blue sky. Neither family quarrel nor a girl were involved. On his dying son, the father found an amulet from Hugentobler. Opening the leather pouch and pulling out an inscribed piece of paper, he read, "This soul belongs to the devil." This evidenced the magician's use of black magic to effect the notable cure.[20]

Such a sinister trafficker in diabolical miracle reminds us of

Simon of Samaria who "used sorcery, and bewitched the people of Samaria" (Acts 8:9); and Bar-jesus, the false prophet and sorcerer of Paphos in Cyprus (Acts 13:8-10). Such emissaries of Satan were the magicians of ancient Egypt, Jannes and Jambres (2 Timothy 3:8), who withstood Moses (Exodus 7:11, 12, 22; 8:7; 9:11). Ancient and modern pagan religions, as well as gross perversions of Christianity, have produced such psychically endowed mediums who have improved their diabolic gift by the study and practice of the "magical arts" (Acts 19:19; cf. Deuteronomy 18:10-14).

In the heathen country of Tibet, which has resisted Christian missions longer than any other land, we can find demon power almost unhindered in occult religion and exhibited in magical arts and diabolic feats. Researchers and missionaries affirm the enormous occult gifts of many priests of the Taschi Lama and especially the so-called red-hooded monks.[21] These priest-magicians are famous for their feats in black magic and especially in telekinesis (table lifting), levitation, materialization, and physical healing.

White magic

The deceptiveness of white magic. White magic is black magic in pious masquerade. It uses, in a magic way, the name of God, Christ, and the Holy Spirit, along with Bible phrases and terminology, but is demonic in character. It is carried on in many so-called Christian circles, especially in areas of rampant cultism or where sound Bible teaching is lacking and the participants are not aware of its demonic nature (cf. 1 Timothy 4:1, 2; 1 John 4:1, 2). It is called "white" because it parades under the banner of light, in contrast to "black" magic that openly enlists the aid of the powers of darkness.

White magic furnishes a perfect illustration of the Apostle Paul's warning: "And no marvel; for Satan himself is transformed into an angel of light. Therefore, it is no great thing if his ministers also be transformed as the ministers of righteousness; whose end shall be according to their works" (2 Corinthians 11:14, 15).

White magic comes into play and alien spirits "not of God" (1 John 4:1) begin to operate when the truth of God is perverted. The Christian's only sure protection against deception by "spirits not of God" is found in Christ through the Bible, rightly understood, believed, and implicitly obeyed (1 John 4:1-3).

Many Christians understand that people who knowingly reject God's revealed truth and espouse flagrant apostasy expose themselves to demonic deception and even serious occult involvement, as happened to the late Bishop James A. Pike.[22] But many Christians do not understand that well-meaning, utterly sincere believers can come under the spell of white magic and demonic influence through deviation from Bible truths, especially the truths regarding the absolute sufficiency of Christ's redemptive work. The acid test for spirits who are "not of God" centers in the Person and full salvation of Christ (1 John 4:1-3).

The spirit realm of good in which the Spirit of God operates is closely related, although distinctly separate, from the spirit realm of evil where Satan and demons operate. If satanic and demonic deception is to be avoided, strict adherence to the truth of God's Word must be maintained (Ephesians 6:11-18). Artful aping by demons of the work and gifts of the Spirit are inevitable, demanding keen exercise of the gift of discerning spirits (cf. 1 Corinthians 12:10).

White magic versus biblical faith and prayer. In biblical faith, trust is placed solely in the Lord Jesus. In white magic it is deflected to someone else (the human agent) or to something else (one's own faith, etc.). In the biblical prayer of faith, the praying person subjects himself to the will of God. In white magic the help of God is demanded under the assumption that exercising such power is in accordance with God's will. In white magic the Christian markings are mere decorations that camouflage the magical means for knowledge or power.

The person who prays in true faith is under the Holy Spirit's inspiration. The white magician is inspired by spirits not of God.

Neutral magic

Besides black and white magic, some authorities distinguish what they call "natural" or "neutral" magic. This category is not supposed to be related to demonism but confined to the natural realm. Doctors of the psychosomatic school believe they can use forces of nature for healing purposes. An instance is furnished by the experience of a young minister who was afflicted with many warts on his hand. He asked a doctor and professor of a class in psychosomatic diseases how he might remove these ugly blemishes. The answer was: "There is only one proven method, namely, charming." This was tried and proved completely effective in removing the warts.[23]

Just like the black and white variety, so-called neutral magic is also the devil's work (except, of course, the mere sleight-of-hand of the magic trickster).

Mental suggestion

Magic and telepathic phenomena. Mental suggestion is the transference of one person's thoughts to another without speech or sounds. It is a form of telepathy in which "knowledge can be acquired without the help of the senses."[24]

While spontaneous telepathic phenomena have no overt occult connections and do not psychically affect those who experience them,[25] cultivation may develop psychic bondage or disturbance and seemingly indicate demonic connections. Magic, in any case, increases telepathic powers and makes mental suggestion a dangerous practice. Evidence is available that "continued experimentation with telepathic tests can cast the experimenter off psychic balance."[26] It is also true that magical practitioners can enslave their victims both morally and financially through mental suggestion.[27]

Criminal hypnosis

Normal and magical hypnosis. Normal hypnosis legitimately practiced by medical men of integrity can have a beneficial purpose. But in the hands of immoral and unscrupulous practitioners, hypnosis can become criminal. The record shows that such dishonest professional men have sexually abused women and girls under hypnosis, their victims being entirely unconscious of the act while it was in progress.[28] Conscience, which is affected by education, religious attitudes, and character traits, is muted as a regulator in the state of hypnosis. Under such conditions impulses can rise up from the subconscious mind and be exploited by unscrupulous people.

Besides professional hypnosis for legitimate medical or psychiatric purposes, there is questionable lay or nonprofessional hypnosis. Such charlatanry can cause much evil, especially when it is connected with occult practices and becomes magical hypnosis. This last variety of hypnosis has far-reaching effects. It may afflict the patient with unclean or blasphemous thoughts, aversion to prayer and religious things in general, anxiety hysteria, etc.

In his spare time a minister studied magic hypnosis as well as magic charming, laying cards, and use of the pendulum. He experimented with these occult phenomena on his wife. As his magical abilities developed, both his and his wife's dislike for prayer and the Word of God increased. His wife also became victimized by very serious anxiety-hysteria, which upset her whole emotional and mental stability.[29]

A lay magic hypnotist who was a student of the *Sixth and Seventh Books of Moses* exercised demonic hypnotic powers over a woman and compelled her strongly against her will to do things she abhorred, such as stealing and adultery. Through pastoral help, the lay hypnotist was led to see the wickedness of his occult art and was persuaded to burn the magic book and abandon his occult practices. His victim was relieved, the occult connections were broken, and she no longer had a compulsive inclination to theft and adultery. Nevertheless, she had a long battle to overcome resistance against God's Word and instability of faith. It took a whole year of prayer on the part of others and a struggle on the victim's part to get completely free of all occult bondage.[30]

Magical mesmerism

Nonmagical curative mesmerism. "Mesmerism" was taught by the Austrian mystic and scientist, Franz Mesmer (1734-1815). According to him a healthy person can charge himself magnetically from the magnetic force fields of the earth, and then by stroking sick people with his hand can exert a healing influence upon them. Mesmer's concept was taken up by the English physician Braid, who declared that the healing force was not magnetic but psychic and called it hypnosis. Those holding to hypnotism contend that human magnetism is only a pre-stage of hypnotism.[31] Whether purely magnetic or a pre-stage to the hypnotic, curative magnetism or mesmerism appears to be an ethically neutral power of nature.[32] However, it is limited, being sufficient for three or at most four patients daily. Then the power is exhausted and must be newly recouped.

Magical curative mesmerism. Natural curative magnetism (like hypnosis) can be greatly intensified by resorting to the occult. Healing magnetizers are constantly tempted to do this for financial reasons, since natural healing magnetism soon becomes used up and must be replenished. Three or four patients daily cannot provide a substantial income or build up one's reputation as a successful healer. For this reason many healing magnetizers turn to other methods. Magic is added to medical magnetism, and religious words and Christian pretensions are used to conceal the demonic nature of their powers. Treatment at their hands may bring a physical cure but, when this occurs, occult bondage or a form of demonic subjection will result.

A young theological student fell under the influence of a strong psychic magnetizer and became the victim of depressions, isolated compulsive images, and strong antipathy toward

God's Word, despite the fact that he was a candidate for the ministry. Prayer became impossible. Psychiatric examination brought no relief, for the underlying cause of the trouble was demonic. Only after eight months of Christian counseling was the victim of magical magnetism liberated from occult bondage.[33]

It is noteworthy that mesmerizers cannot help Christians against their will. The occult mesmerizer himself can discern a situation of this kind and fully realizes his inability to work against the power of God's Spirit. The same thing is true of a spiritistic medium when a praying Christian is present. The fact illustrates the power of the Holy Spirit in restraining evil (cf. 2 Thessalonians 2:6-10).

The ritual of magic

Magic in all of its forms and ceremonies has all the features of a diabolical religion. By demonic dynamic, it attempts to imitate the work of the Holy Spirit and mimics the true Christian faith. The knowledge and power it imparts are satanic counterfeits of the knowledge and power of God.

Magic liturgy versus Christian worship. A magic ceremony commonly involves the use of four elements — invocation, charm, symbolic action, and a fetish. In the case of white magic, the invocation is addressed to God the Father, God the Son, and God the Holy Spirit. If black magic is involved the invocation is addressed to Satan and demonic powers. Such invocation is the counterpart of calling upon God through the Lord Jesus Christ. The invocation of black magic is commonly fortified by a pact with Satan in which the person signs himself over to the devil with his own blood.[34]

The charm, which conjures the magic powers into operation, is the counterpart of the Word of God and prayer. The symbolic action, which is multifarious, mimics biblical symbolic action such as forms of prayer or imposition of hands in prayer. The use of a fetish, which may be defined as a magically charged object, seems to ape the use of water in baptism or bread and wine in the communion supper.

The magic charm. Examples of charms taken from *The Sixth and Seventh Books of Moses* are (1) the transference charm of black magic. Boil the flesh of a swine in the urine of an ailing person, then feed this concoction to a dog. As the dog dies, the ailing person will recover. (2) A healing charm of white magic. Eat, unread, some walnut leaves inscribed with a Bible text. (3) A fertility charm of white magic. Place a woman's hair between two loaves of bread and feed this to cattle while saying a magic verse.

Magical symbolism and fetish. Magic symbolism is intended to give effectiveness to the magic charm and bring about occult transference. Magic symbolism, in turn, is supported by a fetish. This is a magically charmed object which is supposed to carry magical power. Any object, of the most bizarre character, can become a fetish by being magically charmed. The magical effectiveness of the fetish (amulet or talisman) is increased by inscriptions, particularly by magic charm formulas.

An example of fetishism is reported by a German pastor, Rev. Samuel Keller, regarding Frau Brandstätter.[35] This woman was the victim of daily spells during which a male voice spoke out of her body in fluent High-German. Moreover, during these attacks her character was completely altered. From a humble, modest, friendly person she was suddenly transformed into a surly, rude, and unfriendly individual with dreadful strength.

One day, Pastor Keller noticed a tiny leathern pouch suspended from her neck. He grasped it to snatch it away, when the male voice, simulating the voice of a well-known gypsy, Elkimo, cried out, "Don't give up that sack!" Nevertheless, the pastor jerked it off. The spell immediately subsided, and the woman was completely cured. In the little sack they found an inscribed charm, "I am he that holds the seven agues in hand and can send out the seven powers, and if you will hide this and live in my name, you will succeed in all things, and I will protect you." Frau Brandstätter admitted that a few years previously she had bought the amulet from a gypsy. Obviously, the superstitious use of such a magically charmed object elicited unusual demonic activity.

Magical books and literature. Some books devoted to magic are as significant to the magician as the Bible is to the Christian. Perhaps the most influential and widely circulated one — at least in Europe — is the so-called *Sixth and Seventh Books of Moses.* This wicked treatise is falsely ascribed to Moses and attributes his God-given powers to magic (cf. Exodus 7:8, 9; 9:23). This deceptive work seeks to elevate Moses as the patron saint of all magicians.

The *Sixth Book* demonstrates how man can enter into relationships with Satan. The *Seventh Book* instructs those so related how they can achieve dominion through magic over all powers in earth, heaven, and hell. People who possess these books and carry out their instructions pay dearly for their folly by becoming slaves of the devil (Exodus 20:3-5). The diabolical knowledge and power they gain are paid for by tragedy, misery, and every type of occult oppression.[36]

Other popular and widespread magic treatises (especially in Germany, France, and Switzerland) are: *The Little Book of Romanus, The Black Raven, Saint's Blessing, The Genuine Fiery Dragon, Enchanted Words of Black Forest* and *The Eighth to Thirteenth Books of Moses, The Spring Book,* and *The Spiritual Shield.*

The application of magic

Since magic is part of Satan's worldwide program, it is used in numerous and varied areas. God, Christ, the Holy Spirit, and the angels are not the only targets. Men, animals, and inanimate matter provide a target as well. Magic operates mostly for defense against attack, stirring up love and hate, causing the death of animals and human beings, and healing and producing sickness.

Casting and breaking of spells. A spell is produced by the release of demonic power through hypnosis, magnetism, mesmerism, or some other form of magic resulting in an extrasensory influence. Conjurers, charmers, and others who dabble in both white and black magic frequently know how to cast and break spells. They can paralyze a person on the spot, cause a thief to be frozen in his tracks. A Swiss mesmerizer can cast his patients in a spell and force them to return to pay his fee if they forgot to do so.[37]

Although both black and white magic use numerous other enchantments, yet the very heart of both branches centers in casting and releasing the spell.[38] A spell can cause temporary blindness, deafness, dumbness, torpor, sickness, pain, etc. The symptoms will disappear when the spell is broken. Often only superstitious claims are made which remain devoid of reality. But through a genuine magic spell diabolic power is released and real results are obtained. Till the power is recalled or counteracted, the spell remains binding.

Persecution of enemies and defense against attack. Casting and breaking of spells is closely connected with the persecution of hated persons and defense tactics. In this sphere of magic, as it relates to human experience, the most bizarre cases have been observed. In parts of rural Europe where magic has been studied and practiced for centuries, strange phenomena have been reported such as milking cattle dry, or the braiding of horses' tails by an enemy using persecution magic and who has no physical access to perform such a feat naturally.[39] Defense magic often follows the strange formulas outlined in various books on magic, which many German and Swiss families have possessed and followed for generations.

Stirring up love and hate. This category is closely associated with persecution and defense magic. A girl who had trusted Christ in an evangelistic campaign in Germany became the victim of such magic. A man who possessed a great deal of occult literature and practiced magic resented the girl's zeal and determined to silence her. He threatened to cast a spell upon her which would upset her mentally. Indeed, after a few weeks this girl developed psychic disturbances and sought pastoral counseling.[40] Many charms are used to stir up love or hate, and some magicians specialize in this area of magic.

Causing the death of human beings and animals. This type of black magic belongs to the darkest sphere of occultism. The death spells cast by witch doctors among aboriginals (such as the Papuans of New Guinea) provide ample illustration.

Few people are aware that such things are still practiced in parts of Europe today. A woman who engaged in black magic through *The Sixth and Seventh Books of Moses, The Spring Book* and *The Spiritual Shield,* furnishes a good example. She boasted she had done away with her husband and daughter and could persecute her enemies by inflicting various diseases upon them. In honest moments she admits her own life is a tragedy and confesses: "I don't want to do what I am driven to do. But I must do it. The devil drives me. I can never find rest."[41]

So common are various spells cast upon animals that European magicians speak of "stable magic." A black-magic expert was able to kill a cow in four days. A most amazing instance of the use of persecution magic to kill a neighbor's pigs (thirty-two over a period of several years) comes from a farm near Zurich, Switzerland. The perpetrator of this deed was a magician who bound himself to the devil in his own blood and practiced magic according to *The Sixth and Seventh Books of Moses.*[42] Such episodes may appear utterly absurd and pure superstition to people in countries comparatively free of black magic, but instead they should be warnings of the power of Satan and demons where occult literature lures readers into illicit knowledge (cf. Acts 19:19; 2 Thessalonians 2:8-10).

Healing and inflicting sickness. Magical conjurers cannot only heal, they can also inflict physical and mental disorders upon their dupes. In fact, even healing through occult involvement leads to psychic disturbances, as Kurt Koch has observed in innumerable cases of counseling.[43]

A fifteen-year-old girl suffered from tuberculosis inflammation of the hip joint. Since medical help brought no cure, the mother decided to resort to magic. The nurse advised the mother against such a course, but the mother persisted. In anxiety the nurse went to the village pastor for help. The pastor unfortunately was not aware of the serious issues involved and viewed the visit to the magic healer as so much humbug and superstition. Consequently the visit was made, and the "humbug" promptly helped. The girl improved. But, alas, at what a price! Healings by magic simply shift the trouble from the organic to the psychic, thereby releasing the sick condition to a higher level. The girl became psychically disturbed.[44]

The infliction of sickness may be a form of persecution magic. Those adept in the black arts can afflict both the body and mind of their enemy. The victims who believe and trust in magic can in turn use counter-charms. Real deliverance, however, can only be achieved through the gospel of Christ and faith in his conquest over all the powers of darkness.

The effects of magic

The principle of compensation. Magic as the release of special power by satanic and demonic forces is evil in its character and effects. While divine help and miracles produce new strength and positive results, magic weakens faith in God and destroys the right relationship of the creature to the Creator. Magic grants only deceptive aid, shifting the burden to another area. Small relief in one area must be paid for by terrible burdens in another. The principle of compensation prevails. The price exacted is always found to be much greater than the amount of help received. Satan drives a hard bargain and grossly cheats his victims.

The cruelty and bondage of demonic domination. Usually violence, suicide, and insanity will run through a whole family line, where the magical arts have been cultivated and practiced. Such tragic events often involve as many as four generations (cf. Exodus 20:5). Many occultists and magic workers, especially those who have cultivated the black arts and signed themselves over to the devil in their own blood, die horrible deaths. This is especially true when a ready successor is not provided to carry on the nefarious practice. The psychic bondage and oppression that traffickers in occultism themselves suffer, as well as their dupes, is horrifying to contemplate.[45]

Deliverance from magic

Magic is not a disease but the operation and influence of demon powers. To recognize the connection between demonism and magic, it is necessary to know what the Bible has to say about it.

Faith in the triumph of Christ over evil powers. Christian counseling with the victims of occultism demonstrates that Christ conquers the effects of magic completely. "For this purpose the Son of God was manifested, that he might destroy the works of the devil" (1 John 3:8). Christ "hath delivered us from the power of darkness" (Colossians 1:13). "If the Son therefore shall make you free, ye shall be free indeed" (John 8:36). When faith is anchored in Christ's redemptive work, the occultly subjected person is on the way to complete deliverance.

Confession and renunciation of all connections with occultism. A full and clean confession of all occult complicity, together with a prayer of complete renunciation, is essential for deliverance. In severe cases of magic involvement, the counselor must often command the ousting of Satan and evil spirits in the name of Jesus Christ. Frequently fasting and earnest intercessory prayer for the deliverance of the subjected person are mandatory (cf. Matthew 17:21).

Consistent walk of faith. The liberated person must maintain fellowship with the Lord in prayer, separation from evil, and study of the Word. The believer must use the whole armor of God against the powers of evil (Ephesians 6:10-20). He must rely on "the weapons" which "are not carnal, but mighty through God" to the pulling down of Satan's strongholds (2 Corinthians 10:4).

NOTES
CHAPTER 5

1. I. Mendelsohn, "Magic, Magician," *The Interpreter's Dictionary of the Bible,* vol. K-Q (1962), p. 223.
2. *The Babylonian Creation Epic,* Tablet 1, 60-70.

3. *Ibid.,* Tablet 4, 61.

4. *Ibid.,* Tablet 4, 21-29.

5. J. B. Pritchard, *Ancient Near Eastern Texts,* rev. ed. (1955), p. 148b; cf. G. Contenau, *La Magic chez les Assyriens et les Babyloniens.*

6. H. Kaupel, *Die Dämonen im Alten Testament;* A. Guillaume, *Prophecy and Divination.*

7. See "Magic," *Encyclopaedia Britannica,* 14 (1964): 624.

8. *Ibid.* Cf. J. G. Frazer, *The Golden Bough,* vols. 1, 2, and *The Magic Art,* 3rd ed. (1911); R. R. Marett, *Threshold of Religion.* A full bibliography is included in T. Witton Davies, *Magic, Divination and Demonology Among the Hebrews and Their Neighbors,* pp. XI-XVI.

9. Davies, "Magic, Magician," *The International Standard Bible Encyclopedia,* 3 (1939): 1963.

10. See chapters 3 and 4.

11. Kurt E. Koch, *Between Christ and Satan,* p. 73.

12. *Ibid.*

13. Hobart E. Freeman, *Deliverance from Occult Oppression and Subjection,* p. 36. Cf. Kurt Seligman, *The History of Magic;* Elbee Wright, *Book of Legendary Spells;* Arkon Daraul, *Witches and Sorcerers.*

14. Koch, *Between Christ and Satan,* pp. 81, 82. Cf. Rollo Ahmed, *The Black Art;* Lewis Spence, *Encyclopedia of Occultism.*

15. For a discussion of magical blood pacts with examples from counseling experiences, see Kurt E. Koch, *Christian Counseling and Occultism,* pp. 127-130. For the moral degeneracy such initiation into devil cults leads to, see Brad Steiger, *Sex and Satanism.*

16. Koch, *Between Christ and Satan,* pp. 79, 80. Cf. Gerald B. Gardner, *Witchcraft Today;* Robert Goldston, *Satan's Disciples.*

17. See "Black Art," *Encyclopedia Americana,* 4 (1951): 32.

18. This is the conclusion of Professor Paul Diepgen in his book *Medizin und Kultur* (Stuttgart: Ferdinard Enke-Verlag, 1938), pp. 150 ff. Cf. A. L. Constant, *History of Magic;* Andrew Lang, *Magic and Religion;* Lynn Thorndike, *Place of Magic in the Intellectual History of Europe;* Elbiquet (pseudonym), *Textbook of Magic.* In a brief comprehensive survey of magic practice, see "Magic," *The New International Encyclopedia,* 14 (1928): 645-650.

19. Koch, *Christian Counseling,* pp. 121, 122. On occult means to counteract black magic spells cf. Steiger, pp. 163-172. Cf. also C. H. Wallace, *Witchcraft in the World Today.*

20. Koch, *Between Christ and Satan,* p. 91. Cf. Montague Sommers, *The History of Witchcraft.*

21. Cf. Enno Nielsen, ed., *Das Grosse Geheimnis,* p. 141. Although Buddhism entered Tibet in the 8th century A.D., it was strongly influenced by divination, black magic, and sorcery coupled with human sacrifices that characterized the indigenous religion called Bönism. The resulting syncretism was strongly demonic; Clarence C. Hamilton, "Buddhism," *Encyclopaedia Britannica,* 4 (1964): 357.

22. Jess Stearn, well-known reporter on psychic phenomena and author of *Edgar Cayce, the Sleeping Prophet* (an account of the activities of a famous medium), describes Bishop Pike's alleged spirit communication with his dead son (a suicide) in "Bishop Pike's Strange Séances," *This Week, The Baltimore Sun,* January 28, 1968, pp. 4, 5, 13.

23. Koch, *Between Christ and Satan,* p. 97. See Elbee Wright, *Book of Legendary Spells;* Steiger, pp. 105-113.

24. J. B. Rhine, *Die Reichweite des menschlichen Geistes* (Stuttgart: Deutsche Verlagsanstalt, 1950), p. 41.

25. For examples of spontaneous telepathy see Koch, *Christian Counseling,* pp. 45, 46.

26. *Ibid.,* p. 48.

27. For examples see Koch, *Between Christ and Satan,* pp. 85, 86.

28. *Ibid.,* pp. 82-84. Cf. Robert Potter, "Hypnotism Is a Valuable Medical Tool. Can It Be Used for Crime Too?" *Johns Hopkins Journal,* 4, no. 3 (January 1970): 5.

29. Koch, *Between Christ and Satan,* pp. 84, 85.

30. Koch, *Christian Counseling,* p. 95.

31. Rudolf Tischner, *Ergebnisse Okkulter Forschung,* p. 35. See Franz Mesmer, *Encyclopaedia Britannica,* 15 (1964): 287. Mesmer was ordered to leave Austria because medical men thought he was practicing magic.

32. E. Modersohn, *Im Banne des Teufels,* pp. 66, 67.

33. Koch, *Christian Counseling,* pp. 102, 103.

34. For examples of blood pacts made with Satan, see Koch, *Christian Counseling,* pp. 127-130. For examples of spells, hexes, and charms, see Steiger, pp. 99-113.

35. See Samuel Keller, *Aus meinem Leben* (Leipzig: Walter Loepthien, n. d.).

36. Koch declares, "In the many cases which the pastor-counselors have come to know, there is no possessor of *The Sixth and Seventh Books of Moses* who has no psychic complications" (*Christian Counseling,* p. 134). Little wonder that this is so when the following compact is found in the book: "To whatever person possesses this book at any given time, Lucifer makes promise to carry out his commands, but only as long as he possesses the book" (6:6).

37. Koch, *Between Christ and Satan,* pp. 103, 104. Cf. Seligman, *The History of Magic* for the ramifications of magical art.

38. K. Schmeing, *The Second Vision in Nether Germany — The Core of the Reality* (Leipzig: Ambrosius Barth Publications, 1937), p. 137.

39. Koch, *Christian Counseling,* pp. 149, 150.

40. Koch, *Between Christ and Satan,* p. 101.

41. *Ibid.,* pp. 105, 106.

42. For a full account of this exercise of pig-killing magic, see Koch, *Between Christ and Satan,* pp. 174-178. That there are black magicians in Canton Toggenburg who can kill pigs, horses, and other

cattle through their wicked art is well known by local villagers in this part of Switzerland.

43. Koch, *Christian Counseling,* p. 162.
44. *Ibid.,* p. 160.
45. For those who surrender themselves to worship and serve Satan, the moral degradation and perversion are horrifying, as Steiger shows, pp. 7-184.

Demons and Demon Possession

The term "demon possession" does not appear in the Bible. Apparently it originated with the Jewish historian, Flavius Josephus, in the first century A.D.[1] and then passed into ecclesiastical language. The New Testament, however, frequently mentions demoniacs. They are said to "have a spirit," "a demon," "demons," or "an unclean spirit." Usually such unhappy victims of evil personalities are said to be "demonized" (*daimonizomenoi*), i.e., they are subject to periodic attacks by one or more inhabiting demons, who derange them physically and mentally during the seizure.

Rationalistic criticism has persistently denied the reality of demon possession as presented so vividly in the Bible accounts of our Lord's earthly ministry. The mythical theory, advanced notably by Germany's David Strauss, views the whole narrative of Jesus' demon expulsions as purely symbolic, without actual foundation in fact.[2] Demon possession is represented as a vivid symbol of the prevalence of evil in the world, and the expulsion of demons as a corresponding figure of Christ's triumph over it.

Other critics attempt to dismiss demon possession with theories of accommodation or hallucination. The proponents of the first hypothesis declare our Lord simply adapted himself to popular beliefs and terminology without committing himself to the existence or nonexistence of the phenomena described or the truth or falsity of current belief.[3]

The proponents of the second theory consider demon possession a pure hallucination or psychological delusion.[4] But all such views fail to meet the issue. Nor can present-day parapsychologists and psychiatrists, who refuse to recognize evil supernaturalism in the phenomenon of demon possession, either explain it or deal adequately with it.

What is demon possession?

Definition of demon possession. Demon possession is a condition in which one or more evil spirits or demons inhabit the body of a human being and can take complete control of their victim at will. By temporarily blotting out his consciousness, they can speak and act through him as their complete slave and tool. The inhabiting demon (or demons) comes and goes much like the proprietor of a house who may or may not be "at home." When the demon is "at home," he may precipitate an attack. In these attacks the victim passes from his normal state, in which he acts like other people, to the abnormal state of possession.

The condition of the afflicted person in the "possessed" state varies greatly. Sometimes it is marked by depression and deep melancholy, sometimes by vacancy and stupidity that resemble idiocy. Sometimes the victim may be ecstatic or extremely malevolent and wildly ferocious. During the transition from the normal to the abnormal state, the victim is frequently thrown into a violent paroxysm, often falling to the ground unconscious, foaming at the mouth with symptoms similar to epilepsy or hysteria.

The intervals between attacks vary greatly from an hour or less to months. Between attacks, the subject may be healthy and appear normal in every way. The abnormal or demonized stages can last a few minutes or several days. Sometimes the attacks are mild; sometimes they are violent. If they are frequent and violent, the health of the subject suffers.

Distinguishing mark of demon possession. The chief characteristic of demon possession or demonomania is the *automatic projection of a new personality in the victim.* During attack the victim's personality is completely obliterated, and the inhabiting demon's personality takes over completely. The inhabiting demon uses the victim's body as a vehicle for his own thoughts, words, and acts. The demon even speaks out of the victim's mouth and declares emphatically that he is a demon. Frequently he gives his name and dwelling place.

The new personality reveals itself in a different voice and sometimes uses a different language or dialect on a completely different educational or cultural level. Pronouns are used to emphasize the new personality. The first personal pronoun consistently designates the inhabiting demon. Bystanders are addressed in the second person. The victim is referred to in the third person and looked upon during the attack as unconscious and for all practical purposes as nonexistent during this interval.

Demon possession versus insanity. Demonomania should be clearly differentiated from the insanity in which a person imagines himself to be someone else, often a famous personality such as Julius Caesar or Abraham Lincoln. The demoniac, when in the demonized state characterized by the new personality, speaks and acts in all respects like a completely different person. By contrast, the insane person is his own diseased self, his assumed personality being a transparent unreality. In cases of demon possession the new personality clearly and constantly recognizes the distinct existence and individuality of its "possessed" victim, speaking of that victim in the third person, an element entirely lacking in cases of insanity.

Because various inadequate theories have left demon possession largely unexplained, it is quite probable that some patients in mental hospitals are demon possessed rather than insane. This was the conviction of the famous nineteenth-century specialist in mental diseases, Dr. Forbes Benignus Winslow (1810-1874).[5] He correctly recognized the demoniac by a strange duality; and by the fact that, when temporarily relieved from the oppression of the demon, he is frequently able to describe the force which takes control of him and compels him to act and speak shamefully.

Supernatural knowledge and intellectual power of the demon-possessed. While in the demonized state many persons give evidence of knowledge which cannot be accounted for naturally. The demon who takes control of the body of his victim is obviously the source of the superhuman knowledge.

While demon possessed, many persons recognize the Lord Jesus Christ as the Son of God, and display an aversion to and a fear of him (cf. Mark 1:23, 24; 5:7). The remarkable cases of demon possession encountered by John L. Nevius in China during the years 1854-1893 illustrate how common this affliction is in pagan lands. His experiences read like the Gospel accounts.

The case of Mr. Kwo,[6] who lived in Shantung Province, illustrates how a man came under demon domination through worshiping the goddess Wang Mu-niang, wife of the chief divinity of China. A demon appeared to him soon after and said: "I am Wang Mu-niang of Yuinmen san (the name of a nearby mountain). I have taken up my abode in your house." This announcement, made repeatedly by the demon, was the prelude to Mr. Kwo's enslavement to the idol spirit, who drove him to gambling in nearby towns, and then took possession of him as he was returning to his native village. He fell down unconscious, frothing at the mouth, and was carried to his house. The next day in a violent attack he attempted to shoot his father. With the help of neighbors his father bound him with chains and took him to his home some distance away.

A doctor who was called in gave him large doses of medicine to no avail. He left and refused to have anything more to do with the case. For five or six days the victim raved wildly, and his friends were in great distress. In desperation they proposed giving him more medicine. But the demon, speaking through him, replied: "Any amount of medicine will be of no use." His mother then implored, "If medicine is of no use, what shall we do?" The demon replied, "Burn incense to me, and submit yourself to me, and all will be well."

The parents of the victim knelt down and worshiped the demon, imploring him to torment their son no longer. During that time the victim was in a state of complete unconsciousness. A little later when the demon drove the victim to renewed frenzy, his distraught parents repeated their promise to worship and serve him. They also promised that they would urge their son to do likewise. When the son regained consciousness, he reluctantly consented to do so.

The demon gave explicit directions regarding the proposed worship. On the first and fifteenth of each month, incense was to be burned, food offered, and the required prostrations made before the shrine of the goddess, Wang Mu-niang. Periodically the demon came, sometimes every few days, sometimes after a month's lapse. Each time, the victim felt a fluttering of his heart, a sense of overwhelming fear, and inability to control himself. He would quietly ask his wife to fetch a neighboring woman whenever the demon came. The two would burn incense to the demon in the victim's stead and receive his directives, which they then communicated to the possessed.

Although these communications were spoken by the victim's lips, he was completely unaware of them, since he was in the demonized state. The demon often bade the audience not to be afraid, protesting he would not harm them, but rather help them in various ways. He declared he would instruct the victim in the healing art, so that people would flock to him to be cured of their sicknesses. This soon proved true, although many diseases were not under the demon's control. Apparently only those afflicted by evil spirits were completely cured. The victim's long-ill child was not helped.

The demon declared he controlled many inferior spirits. He also frequently outlined his plan for his victim's life and work. He promised he would help him grow more proficient as a healer, and the people would compensate him for his services. Gifts thus earned were to be donated to the nearby pagan temple.

In the summer of 1878, the demon-possessed man heard of the Christian gospel through one of Dr. Nevius' native assistants. After trusting Christ, Mr. Kwo tore down the home shrine and ceased worshiping the demon. The death of his sick child occurred a few days later. In great distress his wife urged him to restore the shrine and resume the worship, believing her daughter's death was caused by the offended de-

mon. But the new Christian remained adamant and refused
to break his vow to worship and trust in Jesus.

A few days later the demon returned and spoke through
his victim to the wife: "I have returned but for one visit.
If your husband is determined to be a Christian, this is
no place for me. But I wish to tell you I had nothing to do
with the death of your child."

"What do you know of Jesus Christ?" she asked. The answer was: "Jesus Christ is the great Lord over all. And now
I am going away, and you will not see me again." "This,"
testified the freed man, "was actually the last visit; we have
not been troubled since." Mr. Kwo faithfully witnessed for
Christ in his village for many years, then emigrated to Central Shantung in 1889. In his new home he continued to be a
faithful witness for Christ, who had delivered him from the
power of the demon.

Demons not only know Christ and his realm, they are experts in their own bailiwick. They share in the cunning subtlety and deception of Satan and carry on his work with great
skill in an effort to blind the minds of unbelievers (cf. 2 Corinthians 4:4).

The possession of extraordinary knowledge always characterizes the demon as he speaks through the body of his victim.
Powers of oratory and poetic expression and the gift of ven-
triloquism are often evidenced. Perhaps the most striking characteristic is the demon's ability to speak languages unknown
by the subject.[7] This is a widespread phenomenon frequently
referred to by Chinese witnesses. In Germany under the ministry of Pastor John Christopher Blumhardt (1805-1880), demons encountered in his prayer cures "spoke in all the different
European languages, and in some which Blumhardt and others present did not recognize."[8]

Supernatural physical strength of the possessed. The victim's new personality often displays not only supernatural
knowledge but supernatural physical strength and other physical alterations as well. Rapid change of facial expression
quickly turns friendliness into a dreadful grimace. A sudden
shift of voice, perhaps from a high soprano to a resounding

bass, introduces the new personality. These psychic transformations are commonly accompanied by a display of tremendous physical strength, often expressed in delirium, wild flailing of hands and feet, and destructive mania endangering those near at hand. Frail women or even children under demon possession can resist three or four strong men. Mr. Kwo at times attacked all who ventured near him.[9]

Reverend H. V. Noyes of the American Presbyterian Mission in Canton, China, reported the case of a native preacher of the London Mission in 1868. While preaching in Fatshan about Jesus casting out demons, Ho-kao was urged by a man to accompany him to his home in a nearby village. His son, a grown man, had been demon possessed for more than ten days, with such show of physical strength that the people had leashed him to a tree like an animal.

Ho-kao went to the village and asked family and friends to kneel down and pray. As soon as the prayer was finished, the chained man gave several mighty leaps in the air, and Ho-kao said: "Take off the chains!" The people were afraid to obey, but Ho-kao took the chains off and led the man quietly into the house, where the victim fell into a peaceful sleep. The family wished to burn incense and continue placating the demon, but were instructed to do nothing of the kind. Instead, the father of the demoniac tore down every vestige of idol worship in the house and renounced paganism completely. He soon joined the church and became a faithful follower of Christ. The demoniac was completely delivered and never had a recurrence of his trouble.[10]

Moral depravity. Another characteristic of demonomania is the complete change of moral character and spiritual disposition of the victim when the new personality is in control. This transformation is due to the nature of the inhabiting demon who completely controls his victim during the demonized state (the attack), and thus manifests his own character.

Just like human beings, demons have different intellectual, moral, and spiritual traits. These traits will manifest themselves accordingly through the possessed person. Some demons are refined, educated, cultured, and even appear to be "good" and benevolent, parading as elect unfallen angels, even as the Holy Spirit himself. Others are unrefined, uneducated, coarse, vile, and morally filthy. The one common attribute of demons is their opposition to Jesus Christ. Outside of this common, central characteristic, various traits are reflected in the conduct of the victim while under attack.

In actual demon possession, which is a crude and gross form of diabolic tyranny, demons of the baser and viler sort seem to operate most freely. Many are notoriously "unclean," and cause their victims to delight in obscenity and nudity while driving them to sexual excesses and moral perversion. This is mostly true in pagan lands both today and during Christ's ministry on earth when demonic opposition was at its highest (Matthew 10:1; Mark 1:27; 3:11; 5:13; 6:7; Luke 4:36; Acts 5:16; 8:7; Revelation 16:13). Demons are not always viciously immoral and unclean. But all spirits who are "not of God" (1 John 4:1-3) always display their essential God-defying and Christ-resisting trait. They always abhor the triune God and the Christian faith. Prayer and the reading of Scripture or some other Christian book upset and excite the inhabiting demon who will then cause his victim to fall into a paroxysm of rage and opposition. Persistence in seeking the true God almost invariably restores the victim to his normal state, often resulting in a permanent cure through the expulsion of the demon. These phenomena appear over and over in biblical accounts of demon possession and also in the history of Christian missions,[11] demonstrating the inadequacy of naturalistic theories of psychiatry and parapsychology to explain them.

Demon possession and spiritism

Affinity of demon possession with spiritistic phenomena. Demon possession is a well-defined phenomenon and should be clearly distinguished from spiritism. Since the same demonic forces are at work in both phenomena, they bear some similar characteristics and result in the same occult oppression and bondage.

The demonized state of the demon possessed is similar to the trance of the spiritistic medium. Both are under the direct influence of demons who speak through them. In the case of the medium who professes to communicate with the spirits of deceased persons, the demon apes the personality and voice of the deceased. In the case of the demon possessed, the evil spirits appear to be more crassly cruel, unclean, violent, and less sophisticated and subtle than spirits working through a clairvoyant medium. In demon possession, they are also more domineering and brutally enslaving.

Nervous muscular reactions and contortions peculiar to the demoniac often appear also in the spiritistic medium when he goes into a trance, but in a much milder form. Then, too, the demoniac is normally an involuntary victim of possession, while the medium is a willing subject, who cultivates psychic propensities and willingly yields to demonic control.

Telekinetic phenomena in demon possession and spiritism. Extraordinary movements of inanimate objects surrounding the demon-possessed remind us of similar happenings in spiritism and magic. Tables, chairs, dishes, and the like are mysteriously moved about without anybody touching them, recalling tumbler moving and table lifting[12] so common in spiritistic séances, and in magic conjurations. In demon possession as well as in spiritism, unexplained rappings and noises in so-called "haunted houses"[13] are heard.

John L. Nevius tells of such a "haunted" house which was rented by a missionary colleague in 1868, in the market town of Changkia-chwang in Shantung Province. The Chinese would not live in it because of the spirits' noisy disturbances. The morning after the Christians moved in, a crowd of curious neighbors inquired how they had slept, and whether they had been disturbed by noises and apparitions during the night.

Although nothing remarkable had occurred to frighten the Christians, the matter did not end there. Before the next night, the occupants of a nearby house came to inform the Christians that a spirit from the house had now taken possession of one of their women. The spirit insisted on taking up its abode with them, since it had been driven away from its former dwelling by the presence of Christians. Such cases of haunted houses abound everywhere in occult literature in connection with mediums, magicians, and demon possessed persons.

Striking is the case of Gottliebin Dittus, a demon-possessed young woman, who became one of Pastor John Christopher Blumhardt's "prayer cures" in the course of his remarkable gospel ministry in nineteenth-century Germany. Gottliebin saw apparitions and had frequent attacks in which she fell unconscious and demons spoke through her in their own voice and personality. Blumhardt and others conversed with them at length.

Pastor Blumhardt opened this case of possession to public scrutiny. He had a woman stay with Gottliebin, and asked a committee of prominent citizens to conduct a thorough investigation. Persons were stationed all around the house, in various rooms, and even in Gottliebin's bedroom. Noises were heard which gradually increased in violence and seemed to concentrate in Gottliebin's chamber. Chairs bounced, windows rattled, plaster fell from the ceiling, and objects moved about without any visible explanation. Prayer caused the noises and phenomena to increase. When the victim was removed to another house to live with another family, the noises and telekinetic phenomena continued for a while in her former residence and then began in the new one.

On one occasion, after continued prayer, one of the demons inhabiting Gottliebin cried out, "All is now lost. Our plans are destroyed. You have shattered our bond, and put everything into confusion. You, with your everlasting prayers — you scatter us entirely. We are 1,067 in number. But there are still multitudes of living men, and you should warn them lest they be like us forever, lost and cursed of God."

Between December 2 and December 28, 1843, complete deliverance from demon possession and restoration to health came to Gottliebin, including the sudden healing of a deformed limb that had not responded to therapy. But the final battle was fearful. Blumhardt, after hours of prayer, commanded the demon to come forth. With a terrible outcry, penetrating to a great distance, the demon confessed that he was an emissary of Satan. Leaving his victim with the piercing yell, "Jesus is Victor!" the evil spirit and hordes of demons under him departed, never to return to their victim.[14] This was the climax of an eighteen-month-old struggle against stubborn demon spirits.

Elijah Bingham, a missionary of the Sudan Interior Mission, relates a harrowing experience that illustrates the strange telekinetic phenomena associated with demonic manifestations among pagan peoples in Africa today.[15] Having preached the gospel and witnessed demon expulsion in a village deep in the forest, he retired alone to a native hut and experienced a night of strange noises by evil spirits. Although he had securely fastened the door of his hut before he retired, the missionary awoke to find the contents of the hut in complete disarray and utter confusion. The amazing and terrifying thing was that the door was still securely fastened. No man or beast had entered. Evil spirits had obviously been at work in a satanic assault against God's servant, who had come to preach the gospel and claim Christ's victory over the powers of darkness.

Healing powers in demon possession and spiritism. It is not uncommon for the controlling demon to promise healing powers to his possessed victim and to grant such supernatural abilities in exchange for worship and yielded service. John Nevius found numerous instances of such transactions in his experiences with the demon possessed of China.[16] Healing is a common phenomenon of spiritism and of both black and white magic.[17]

But if demon powers heal, they also cause diseases. Their object is not to liberate the victim but to deceive and enslave him. They either heal or cause sickness as it furthers their nefarious plans. What is more significant is that even when demons help heal physical diseases, they exact a price either in some type of occult oppression or psychic disturbance in their victim or by causing him to fall a prey to error and false doctrine.[18]

Physical healing, when not according to God's will and for

his glory in answer to prayer, but effected through demonic spirits, always has Satan's costly price tag attached to it. Satan merely shifts the malady from the physical to the mental or emotional. The victim often falls into doctrinal errors of the cult in which the healing occurred. When black magic is used with demonic help, the practice of healing and causing diseases merely fosters satanic cunning and effects no real deliverance.

Spirit-communication in demon possession and spiritism. The controlling demon who speaks out of the body of a possessed victim[19] is similar to the deceiving spirit who apes the dead through a medium.

A missionary, W. E. Wright of West Nigeria, Africa, tells how a demon-possessed witch doctor spoke clairvoyantly, as demons do through a medium. "As I rode on horseback along a country path, I was overtaken by a witch doctor. Curious, as always, I made inquiries as to the contents of the leather bag hung over his shoulder on a miniature axe (the emblem of his profession). He drew from his bag a bundle of papers on which were green and orange markings, an imitation of Arabic writing by an illiterate. He volunteered to read to me from the book, and before I could stop him, for I had seen enough, he began nonsense reading in an ordinary voice. Then suddenly his voice changed. He was possessed, and I heard a demon through his lips telling me that I had a sick little girl in my house. (My daughter had been sick for several days, and as he was a total stranger it was unlikely that he would have heard it.) I silenced him as quickly as I could, reading to him from my Book."[20]

Spirit-invocation in demon possession and spiritism. The invoking or summoning of spirits by means of hymns, prayers, and acts of worship in spiritistic séances, finds a counterpart in demon possession. Often the demon speaking through his victim in the demonized state will demand the burning of incense as well as worship and service.[21] In return he often promises alleviation from torment and powers of physical healing or clairvoyant and prognostic gifts assuring financial income and material prosperity to the enslaved person.[22]

Paganism is replete with fear of demons who must be appeased by worship and servile obedience. Those who accept magical powers of healing and clairvoyance at the hand of demonic powers may escape the grosser torments of vile spirits only to fall under more terrible bondage and become Satan's tools to enslave others.

Demon possession and demon influence

Definition of demon influence. In demon influence, evil spirits exert power over a person short of actual possession. Such influence may vary from mild harassment to extreme subjection when body and mind become dominated and held in slavery by spirit agents. Christians, as well as non-Christians, can be so influenced. They may be oppressed, vexed, depressed, hindered, and bound by demons.

Demon influence and demon possession. Although severe demon influence resembles demon possession, it is never the same. In demon possession one or more evil spirits dwell in a person's body as their house and take complete possession of it at times. In this condition the personality and consciousness of the victim are completely "blacked out," and the personality of the demon takes full control. He thinks, speaks, and acts through the body of the possessed, which he absolutely dominates and uses as if it were his own.

Demon influence, even in its most severe forms, does not manifest the same abject domination by evil spirits that so saliently characterizes actual possession. There is no blacking out of consciousness, no demonized state, no usurpation of the body as a mere tool of the inhabiting demon, no speaking with another voice and the projection of another personality through the victim. In other respects, however, demon influence closely resembles actual possession.

Characteristics of demon influence. Demon influence may occur in different degrees of severity and in a variety of forms, both in Christians and non-Christians. In its less severe forms, demon attack comes from without through pressure, suggestion, and temptation. When such pressure, suggestion, and temptation are yielded to, the result is always an increased degree of demon influence. Although the human race fell in Adam and became a prey to Satan and demons, the forces of darkness have always been severely restricted. They can enslave and oppress fallen man only to the degree he willingly violates the eternal moral law of God and exposes himself to evil (cf. Exodus 20:3-5).

Since fallen man is unable to keep God's moral law perfectly, and is acceptable to God only on the basis of Christ's atonement, all men, saved as well as unsaved, can be subjected to demon influence. The saved, however, have been delivered "from the powers of darkness" and "translated into the kingdom of God's dear Son" (Colossians 1:13). This means that they have been delivered from evil powers. They need to know of this freedom in Christ and act accordingly (cf. Romans 6:11).

Demon influence may manifest itself in blindness and hardness of heart toward the Word of God and the gospel of Christ (2 Corinthians 4:4). It produces antagonism toward God or departure from the faith, resulting in open apostasy (1 Timothy 4:1) or in doctrinal corruption and perversion of the truth, evident in a babel of cults creating Christian disunity (1 John 4:1, 2). Demon influence in doctrine leads to corrupt conduct and practice (1 Corinthians 10:16-22), loving pleasure more than God (2 Timothy 3:4) and indulging in defiling lust (2 Peter 2:10-12). If an orthodox creed is embraced, demon influence may show itself in empty adherence to the letter of the law without the spirit or in ritualistic formalism (2 Timothy 4: 2, 3).

When the moral law of the creature's supreme love and devotion to the Creator is violated by idolatry and occult involvement, the transgressor and his descendants are subjected to more serious enslavement and oppression by demon spirits (Exodus 20:1-5).[23] When the laws of moral purity are ignored (Exodus 20:14; Romans 1:24) the divine restraint is removed and severe demon influence drags men down to moral depravity as the dupes of spirits of lust and uncleanness (Romans 1:26-32). Likewise, when the law of love for one's fellow man is violated, demon power may take hold of a person and goad him on to murder (Exodus 20:13).

A case of severe demon influence came to the author's attention while conducting a spiritual emphasis conference at the Philadelphia College of the Bible in October 1969. After one of my sermons, a twenty-year-old man required private counseling. He was the victim of chronic depression, suicidal mania, and paralyzing fear that had haunted him from childhood. Although he was a good student and an able evangelist, he was at times filled with blasphemous thoughts and afflicted with deep unbelief in the Word of God and the message of salvation. He was so distraught that he refused to reveal his name at the time of counseling. By his own admission, he had been examined by a psychiatrist and given a clean bill of health.

After listening to him, I was eager to find out whether his parents or grandparents had ever dealt in the occult. His reply was an emphatic "Yes!" His paternal grandparents had opposed the marriage of their son, and vented their hatred of his mother upon their grandchild. They sought to curse and kill him by using black magic, in which they were adept. His childhood had been a nightmare of fear, as his mother resorted to protective magic to ward off the effects of the persecution and death magic. She, too, had come under severe demonic enslavement and fear.

This case demonstrates how occult involvement reaches out to children. It also reveals how modern psychology and psychiatry fail to diagnose a case properly when they deny the reality of evil supernaturalism.

We do not know whether such aggravated cases of demon influence go deeper than external pressure, suggestion, and temptation. They apparently do, and demonic invasion of the body seemingly is involved and the personality is infested by one or more vile spirits. These demons, however, act more like visitors or guests in a home than the owners of the house, as is the case in demon possession. In the latter case the demons possess the property and reside there permanently, always having ready access and full control of the premises to do with as they please. In addition, there is the dual personality of the victim in the demonized state, which is never true of demon influence alone.

Demon influence and Christian disobedience. Although the believer is safe and secure in his position "in Christ," before God, he should not abuse the privilege. Persistent disobedience to God's will and other sins may result in "a sin unto (physical) death" (1 John 5:16), or to the solemn delivering of "such a one unto Satan for the destruction of the flesh, that the spirit might be saved in the day of the Lord Jesus" (1 Corinthians 5:5).

Whatever else this may mean, it unquestionably points to severe chastening of the saint who becomes guilty of sensualism, gross sin, or some other form of immorality. The purpose of the correction is that the believer "may not be condemned with the world" (1 Corinthians 11:32). Paul's "delivering over to Satan," although apparently a last-resort method of divine dealing with antinomian abuse of grace, does not imply actual demon possession. It does suggest liability to physical and mental sickness, even demonic influence and bondage, and in extreme cases, physical death.

Demon possession and Christian experience

Can a Christian become demon possessed? It is possible for a believer to experience severe demon influence or obsession if he persistently yields to demonic temptation and sin. But most Christians would hesitate to say that a believer can become demon possessed. Such cases are rarely seen, if ever, in the United States. However, in lands where demon-energized idolatry has flourished unchecked by the gospel for ages, new believers who were delivered from demon possession have been known to become repossessed when they return to their old idols.[24] The testimonies of numerous missionaries in pagan areas support this evidence.[25]

In *Biblical Demonology*[26] this author stated: "To demon possession, only unbelievers are exposed."[27] This statement was inferred, since Scripture does not clearly settle the question. It was based on the assumption that an evil spirit could not indwell the redeemed body together with the Holy Spirit.

Since the first publication of *Biblical Demonology* in 1952, the author has received many letters from missionaries all over the world who question the theory that true believers cannot become demon-possessed. They claim to have witnessed cases of repossession among converts from ancient idolatrous cultures, such as in China and India, and also among aboriginal peoples in primitive civilizations, who live in servile fear and abject bondage to Satan and demons.

The claims of these missionaries appear valid, since Christians in enlightened lands where the Word of God and Christian civilization have restrained the baser manifestations of demonism can sometimes become victims of demon influence and oppression.

To what extent can a Christian become occultly oppressed and enslaved? The counseling experience of Dr. Kurt Koch[28] and others has established that occult involvement often results in demonic oppression or subjection that will sometimes affect even the third or fourth generation (cf. Exodus 20:3-5). The family members who become believers can be affected and in need of deliverance even if they have not dealt in the occult.

Believers who persist in flagrant sin may be driven by demons into emotional instability, insanity, or even suicide. Severe demon influence can produce enslavement and subjection even if it does stop short of actual possession. Believers need to heed the warning: "Be composed! Be on your guard! Your accuser, the devil, prowls around like a roaring lion in search of someone to devour" (1 Peter 5:8, Berkeley).

Demon dispossession

Exorcism in pagan lands. Exorcism is the process of expelling evil spirits from persons or places by certain adjurations, incantations, magic acts, and formulas. Among ancient peoples, exorcism depended largely on the efficacy of magical formulas, commonly compounded of the names of deities, and repeated with magic ritual over the bodies of the possessed. Power to expel evil spirits supposedly resided in the words themselves. Therefore, great importance was attached to the correct recital of the right formulas and the meticulous observance of the prescribed ritual. The recovery of important incantation texts and magical papyri from Babylonian, Assyrian, and Egyptian antiquity demonstrates the widespread belief in demon inhabitation and use of exorcisms.[29]

The same prevalence of demon inhabitation has been encountered in the worldwide missionary outreach from about 1750 to the present. The penetration of China, India, Japan, Burma, Ceylon, and other countries with the Christian gospel has revealed the hold of demonism on pagan cultures and the varied methods of exorcism of evil spirits. The same phenomena exist among primitive people of South America, Africa, and the islands of the sea.

Methods of pagan exorcism. Some common methods of exorcism involve the infliction of pain to the one possessed, such as beating, pricking with needles, pinching, and burning.[30] The theory is that spirits seek to inhabit the bodies of men (and also animals) to find a resting place and in some inscrutable way obtain physical gratification. When the demon-possessed is in the demonized state and unconscious, inflicted physical pain or pleasure is supposedly transferred to the possessing spirit. Discomfort will drive him out of his abode.[31]

The celebrated shrine at Ghonspore, India, is famous among both Hindus and Muslims as a place where demons are exorcised. The exorcists have their own methods, but violence and infliction of pain are the most common. When the cure fails, the demon is said to be vicious and obstinate. If severe beating of the victim proves fruitless, cotton wicks soaked in oil are lighted and stuffed up the nostrils.[32]

A young woman of India named Melata sank into deep melancholy and became demon possessed after the death of both her parents. Taken to the shrine at Ghonspore, she was treated first by beating, questioning, and enchantments. When these methods failed, she was tied and lighted wicks steeped in oil were stuffed up her nostrils and into her ears. This succeeded in exorcising the demon, and she was restored.[33] The history of paganism is replete with bizarre superstition and hideous cruelties. Methods of exorcism used by "witch doctors" among aboriginal peoples also show the utter inhumanity and heartless cruelty of the fear-ridden and demon enslaved.

Jewish exorcism. Even among the ancient Jews, exorcism was tainted with gross polytheistic superstition. In the *Book of Tobit* the heart and liver of a miraculously caught fish are burned upon the ashes of incense. The resulting smell and smoke disgust and drive away a demon.[34] Josephus (A.D. 37-95), the learned Jewish historian, recounts a cure in which a demon was drawn through the nostrils of a demoniac by use of a magic root, allegedly prescribed by Solomon. The effectiveness of the cure became evident when the demon in his hasty exit upset a vessel of water.[35] Rabbinical writers offer no improvement on such fanciful methods of exorcism, influenced by paganism rather than by their own monotheistic faith and sacred Scriptures.[36]

Certainly the Jews of Jesus' day were also under pagan influence when they exorcised demons (Matthew 12:25-29). Some expulsions were no doubt genuine answers to fasting and prayer by sincere Pharisees, but many served Satan's program by their temporary results and protection of the real enemy. Such expulsions do not represent divisions in the satanic kingdom nor instances of "Satan casting himself out," but satanic collaboration to extend his empire of evil (cf. Matthew 12:25; Acts 19:13-17).

Dispossession in the name of Christ. Our Lord's method of expelling demons is in clear contrast to Jewish and pagan exorcisms. As omnipotent Lord of the spirit world, he merely spoke and the demons obeyed. All those who were possessed recognized the lordship of Christ and confessed his power (Mark 1:24, 34; 5:7). He "cast out the spirits with a word" (Matthew 8:16). He did not resort to pagan rituals but his method was completely authoritative and efficient. His were genuine expulsions. He cast out demons "by the Spirit of God," and as a result "the kingdom of God" became evident (Matthew 12:28).

Christ's disciples cast out demons "in the name of Jesus" (Mark 16:17; Luke 10:17). The name stands for the infinite Person behind the name, and does not contain any magical power in itself. When prostituted into a ritualistic rigmarole, however, as in white magic, it becomes a deceiving tool in the hands of Satan's agents to delude the undiscerning by false miracles and spurious healings. Such diabolic miracles do not destroy Satan's kingdom, but build it up. Diabolical exorcism does not produce true dispossession, but a mere reallocation. Demonic healing may relieve physical symptoms, but substitute a psychical ill or doctrinal form of error. This subterfuge explains in part the increase of theological decadence and phenomenal growth of sects and cults within professing Christianity in these latter days.

Dispossession in the name of Christ today. Today's mission fields provide many examples of deliverance from demon possession in the mighty name of Jesus Christ. Mary C. Norton tells of such an experience in India. Under demon control, a young girl insisted she must dance for the missionaries, which she did wildly and uncontrollably and with every evidence of demon possession. She became so violent that the only way to control her was to hold her by the hair. Her violent jerking almost pulled out her hair.

When a Christian worker ordered the demon to leave her in the name of Jesus Christ, the girl ceased her violence, fell to the ground, and lay there as dead for about a minute (cf. Mark 9:26). Then she sat up and pulled the top part of her sari modestly over her face while she was helped to her feet. When asked why she had been lying on the ground, she replied that she did not know. When asked if anyone had pulled her hair, she disavowed any knowledge of it. When the missionary tested her by saying, "Will you dance for me?" she replied, "No, Memsahib, I do not know how to dance." She was sweet, modest, and quiet and completely delivered from the demon that had possessed her.[37]

Major R. P. D. Snow of the Poona and Indian Village Mission, Poona, India, tells of a young woman who frequently fell under the power of an evil spirit who tried to kill her by throwing her into a fire or a well. Everyone who knew her feared that one day she would lose her life when she lapsed into the demonized state and became overpowered with suicidal mania. On one occasion she narrowly escaped death when neighbors pulled her out of a well in the nick of time.

Meanwhile, her husband had become a Christian. Gradually his wife began to understand the Christian gospel. The transformed life of her husband and his evident joy in witnessing for Christ made a profound impression upon her. She concluded that he who had worked such a change in her husband could rescue her from demon possession. She turned to Christ in true faith.

The immediate result was complete deliverance from demonic spirits and a joyful peace she had never supposed existed. Today she is back in the village where she had been known as a demoniac, active with her husband in the service of the Lord, and a testimony to Christ's power to deliver from demonism.[38]

NOTES
CHAPTER 6

1. Alfred Edersheim, *The Life and Times of Jesus the Messiah,* 1: 479.
2. David Friedrich Strauss, *Das Leben Jesu,* Zweiter Band (Tuebingen Verlag Von C. F. Osiander, 1836), pp. 21-52. Most psychologists dismiss the idea of actual demon possession, as T. K. Oesterreich, *Possession, Demoniacal and Other Among Primitive Races in Antiquity, the Middle Ages, and Modern Times.*
3. Cf. A. A. Hodge, *Outlines of Theology,* p. 257.
4. Cf. John Owen, "The Demonology of the New Testament," *Bibliotheca Sacra and Biblical Repository XVI* (January 1859), pp. 124, 125. For a present-day defense of the fact that the Gospels are dominated by the conviction that this world is to some undefined degree in bondage to Satan and demonic powers, see James Kallas, *Jesus and the Power of Satan,* pp. 1-215.
5. Cf. Dr. Winslow's valuable work, *Obscure Diseases of the Brain and Disorders of the Mind,* 4th ed. (1860, 1868). Cf. also G. R. Pember, *Earth's Earliest Ages and Their Connection with Modern Spiritualism and Theosophy,* pp. 261, 262; W. Menzies Alexander

M. D., *Demon Possession in the New Testament*: *Its Relations Historical, Medical, and Theological*, p. 172.

6. John L. Nevius, *Demon Possession* (reprint ed., 1968), pp. 17-27.

7. *Ibid.*, p. 58. For a general presentation of demonic phenomena see Paul Bauer, *Wizards That Peep and Mutter*, pp. 5-160.

8. Nevius, p. 115. One wonders whether the speaking in tongues in Father Divine's Peace Mission Movement founded about 1930 is of such a demonic variety. This is difficult not to believe when the founder of the sect claimed to be God himself. Cf. R. W. Parker, *Incredible Messiah*; Sara Harris, *Father Divine*.

9. Cf. also Nevius, pp. 23, 53. Verna Pullen, Jos, Nigeria, West Africa, tells about a frail sixteen-year-old demon-possessed boy who could scarcely be held down by four men; see *Demon Experiences in Many Lands,* pp. 106, 107.

10. Nevius, pp. 76-78. For a remarkable case of deliverance from demon possession by protracted prayer on the part of a group of Christians today, see A. J. MacMillan, *Modern Demon Possession,* pp. 3-5.

11. Nevius, pp. 9-194. Cf. *Demon Experiences in Many Lands,* pp. 7-128, which draws on modern eyewitness reports from China, India, Colombia, Korea, Nigeria, Ethiopia, etc., concerning deliverance from "unclean spirits." For the moral perversions to which evil spirits drive their slaves, especially in devil-worshiping cults, see Brad Steiger, *Sex and Satanism,* pp. 7-184.

12. See Kurt E. Koch's discussion of these phenomena in spiritism in *Christian Counseling and Occultism*, pp. 28-41, and *Between Christ and Satan,* pp. 127-129; cf. Kurt Seligman, *The History of Magic.*

13. For a full account see Nevius, pp. 10-12, and for other dramatic illustrations included by Nevius, see pp. 61, 62, 111-116. A present-day parallel is the case of the "haunted" flat of Bishop James A. Pike in Cambridge, England. See James A. Pike and Diane Kennedy, *The Other Side,* pp. 71-95.

14. For a full account of this amazing and thoroughly attested case see Nevius, pp. 111-116. For a similar long and terrific struggle see "Battle With a Possessed Woman," as told by Otto Vogt in Koch's *Between Christ and Satan,* pp. 226-234, and MacMillan, pp. 3-5.

15. See *Demon Experiences in Many Lands,* pp. 11-14.

16. *Ibid.*, pp. 25, 26, 37, 66, 321.

17. See chapter 5 for discussion of magic, and chapter 7, "Demons and Healing."

18. This is the explanation of healings in the cults of Christianity, including spiritism (cf. Raphael Gasson, *The Challenging Counterfeit,* pp. 61-65) as well as in pagan religions. Such a perverted cult as Father Divine's Peace Mission Movement claimed healings, which it is hard to believe do not belong to the demonic category; cf. John Hosher, *God in a Rolls Royce.*

19. Cf. Nevius, pp. 22, 24, 34, 35, 39, 46, 47, 68; MacMillan, pp. 3-5, 16.

20. W. E. Wright, "A Witch Doctor Possessed," in *Demon Experiences in Many Lands,* p. 104.

21. Nevius, p. 24.

22. *Ibid.,* p. 26.
23. Koch, *Christian Counseling,* pp. 153, 162; Hobart E. Freeman, *Deliverance from Occult Oppression and Subjection,* pp. 47, 48. MacMillan gives examples of demon possession of an uninstructed believer as the result of dabbling in spiritism, pp. 3-5, 17.
24. Cf. Nevius, p. 52; Walter Ohman, *Demon Experiences in Many Lands,* p. 79.
25. Cf. Freeman, p. 52.
26. Published by Scripture Press Foundation, Wheaton, Illinois, 9th ed. (1969).
27. *Ibid.,* p. 100.
28. Koch, *Christian Counseling,* pp. 1-162. Believers who either ignorantly or knowingly dabble in spiritism may become obsessed or possibly possessed; cf. MacMillan, pp. 3-5.
29. Morris Jastrow, *Hebrew and Babylonian Traditions,* p. 202; R. W. Rogers, *The Religion of Babylonia and Assyria,* p. 146; T. K. Oesterreich, *Possession Among Primitive Races,* p. 100. Cf. F. F. Ellinwood in his introduction to Nevius' *Demon Possession and Allied Themes,* 5th ed.
30. Nevius, pp. 50-54, 67-72; cf. J. S. Wright, "Possession," *The New Bible Dictionary,* J. D. Douglas, ed., pp. 1010-1012.
31. Nevius, pp. 193, 194.
32. W. Knighton, "Demoniacal Possession in India" in *The Nineteenth Century* (October 1880). For a general discussion of the phenomena connected with demon possession and expulsion, see John Fell, *Demoniacs.*
33. Knighton, *Ibid.*
34. *Tobit* 6:7; 8:2, 3.
35. Flavius Josephus, *Antiquities of the Jews* 8. 2. 5 in *Life and Works of Josephus,* pp. 240, 241.
36. Edersheim, 2: 775, 776.
37. Mary C. Norton, "An Experience in India," *Demon Experiences in Many Lands,* p. 56.
38. Major R. D. P. Snow, "Saved and Delivered," *Demon Experiences in Many Lands,* pp. 77, 78.

Demons and Healing

The Bible warns us that Satanic delusions will abound in the last days. Our Lord himself predicted that false Christs and false prophets would arise and perform many demonic signs and wonders (Mark 13:22) and seduce many. The Apostle Paul warned that "the mystery of iniquity" (2 Thessalonians 2:7) would work throughout the age, but particularly at the end, when many would "give heed to seducing spirits" and thus become ensnared by "doctrines of demons" (1 Timothy 4:1).

The Apostle John also warned against Satan's blandishments as he parades "as an angel of light" (2 Corinthians 11:14). God's people should not allow themselves to be duped by false teachers. "Loved ones, do not put faith in every spirit, but God, for many false prophets have been let out into the world" (1 John 4:1, Berkeley).

The power to heal diseases is frequently manifested in spiritism, magic, and demon possession. The clairvoyant medium often claims that he can heal the body, as well as foretell the future. The magical charmer and mesmerizer can both cure and cause diseases. The person afflicted with an evil spirit is often promised ability to cure physical ailments if he will serve the dominating demon.

Because of the satanic imitation of the genuine "gifts of healing" (1 Corinthians 12:9), it is imperative and of the utmost importance that God's people dismiss the naïve and erroneous notion that all healings are of God. God's children need the gift of "discerning of spirits" (1 Corinthians 12:10) to beware of occult healing methods and similar movements of our day.

Otherwise they run the risk of being seduced by religiously camouflaged acts where the demonic masquerades as the divine.

Healing by divine power

Healing through prayer and faith versus magic. The classic passage of Scripture on this subject is James 5:14-16. "Is any sick among you? Let him call for the elders of the church, and let them pray over him, anointing him with oil in the name of the Lord; and the prayer of faith shall save the sick, and the Lord shall raise him up; and if he have committed sins, they shall be forgiven him. Confess your faults one to another, and pray one for another, that ye may be healed. The effectual fervent prayer of a righteous man availeth much."

This text establishes that healing by God in response to faith and prayer is diametrically opposed to magic healing by spirits not of God. Divine healing requires simple faith in God; magic healing demands superstitious faith in the charmer, healing medium, or magician. In divine healing genuine prayer is offered. In magic, elaborate incantations and magic formulas and rigmaroles are used. In magic, trust is placed in the prescriptions of magical literature and in the magic charms which bring the magic powers into action.

In divine healing, the laying on of hands symbolizes that the man of God is the instrument through which God's power flows. The magic symbolism, which is exceedingly varied and bizarre, underscores that the charm releases the magic power. The use of oil is probably to be thought of as a symbol of the Holy Spirit, the manifestation of divine power, rather than as of therapeutic value (Isaiah 1:6; Luke 10:34). Perhaps the magic counterpart is found in the heathen fetish, which is regarded as a magically charged object or substance.

To claim healing "in the name of the Lord" simply means that it is done through the power of Christ, the Creator-Redeemer. Magic charmers lay great stress upon the efficiency of the magic word, since it is considered a power in itself. But when the magic healer uses God's name and Bible words, they no longer stand for God. The word itself is idolized and the creature is set up against the Creator. But the word isolated from God and the clear directives of the Scriptures falls a prey to demonic power. This is certainly true of unsaved healing practitioners who use the veneer of Christian profession to cloak their magic technique (Matthew 7:21-23).

Healing in the Hebrew-Christian church

The passage in James stands in diametrical contrast to the magical healing procedures of New Testament times and was a warning of the perils of popular cures wrought by the demonic rather than the divine. It inculcates for all time the true method of healing by prayer to God and faith in Christ, yet it cannot be applied today except with the careful distinctions that James included. Unless this is done, the magical and the demonic may ensnare the seeker of "divine healing." The following reasons are offered to show why this is so.

First, James 5:14-16 was not primarily addressed to the Gentile Church. It was written to "the twelve tribes" in the dispersion (James 1:1), that is, to the very earliest Jewish converts to Christ during the transition period (Acts 1:1—9:43). Internal evidence places this Epistle as one of the earliest of all New Testament books to be dated, possibly as early as A.D. 45. The Church order and discipline it displays are simple in the extreme. The leaders are called "teachers" and "elders" with no mention of "bishops" or "deacons." Believers still assembled in the "synagogue" (James 2:2). The Epistle could be described as an interpretation of the Mosaic law and the Sermon on the Mount in the light of the gospel of Christ.

Second, James 5:14-16 is based on the healing covenant made with Israel. This covenant is stated in Exodus 15:26: "If thou wilt diligently hearken to the voice of the Lord thy God, and wilt do that which is right in his sight, and wilt give ear to his commandments, and keep all his statutes, I will put none of these diseases upon thee, which I have brought upon the Egyptians; for I am the Lord that healeth thee." Jewish converts to Christ could invoke this covenant of healing "in the name of the Lord," the Savior-Messiah (James 5:14b), through whom there was also forgiveness of sins and restoration from backsliding (James 5:15).

This healing covenant concerned Israel only, the people of the covenants (Romans 9:5). It followed the Passover, typifying atonement (Exodus 12:1-28). It was accordingly related to redemptive atonement, but cannot be said to be "in the atonement." As a healing covenant it was operative upon Israel from its constitution as God's chosen nation at the exodus until the nation's setting aside in unbelief (Acts 28:23-29), the Epistle of James being written before this climactic event.

When the nation Israel will be saved and restored to national blessing at the second advent (Isaiah 53:1-12) the healing covenant will be reinstated, accompanied by the restoration of miracles of healing and other supernatural powers (Isaiah 35:5, 6; Hebrews 6:5).

Third, James 5:14-16 under the healing covenant with Israel guaranteed early Hebrew Christians instantaneous and complete healing in response to faith in Christ. Healing "in the name" and "through faith in the name" brought such miraculous deliverance as was manifested in the cripple at the Gate Beautiful (Acts 3:6, 16). Such healings among Hebrew Christians were the order of the day until the setting aside of Israel in unbelief and with this event the abrogation of the healing covenant with the nation (Acts 4:30; 5:12-16; 6:8; 8:7, 8).

The use of oil also connects with the Jewish setting of James 5:14-16. Such anointing with oil was a general Jewish practice, as shown by the Talmud. Our Lord and his disciples adopted this custom (Mark 6:13). Many expositors interpret the oil to symbolize the use of natural means on the ground that it was a common medicinal remedy in the ancient Near East (Isaiah 1:6; Luke 10:34). Others see in it a type of God's Spirit by whom the healing was effected.

But the emphasis is upon "the prayer of faith" which "saves," i.e., delivers the physically ill person in the sense of curing him of his malady (cf. Matthew 9:21, 22). This efficacious faith for healing was divinely imparted to the apostolic Jewish Christian elders as they claimed the promises of Israel's healing covenant (Exodus 15:26). But the all-important point for the correctly instructed Christian minister to see, now that the nation Israel and her healing covenant have been set aside while the great Gentile Church is being called out, is that such "prayer of faith" is divinely given and divinely operative in the established Gentile Church only when it is God's will to heal. The Epistles addressed to the Church clearly teach that it is not always God's will to heal, nor is it always for the believer's highest good to be healed. Chastening, testing, molding into Christlikeness, and other factors condition the Lord's healing of a Christian's sicknesses (1 Corinthians 5:1-5; 11:30-32; 2 Corinthians 12:7-9; 1 Timothy 5:23, 2 Timothy 4:20).

This is the reason why nowhere in any of the Church Epistles is anything said about anointing the sick with oil (cf. 2 Corinthians 5:7) and the prayer of faith saving (healing) them. "The prayer of faith," however, does save (heal) them, but it is only given when God's purpose is determined in each case, and such prayer is offered in God's will. For so-called "faith healing"[1] to teach that it is always God's will to heal believers, and to command "God in Jesus' name" to do this is a presumption into which many modern faith healers have fallen.

In the light of a completed redemption and the fullness of the indwelling Spirit now enjoyed, God's New Testament saints are called to walk by faith and not by sight (2 Corinthians 5:7). The nation Israel, with only types and shadows of future redemption, had many signs and evidences of God's presence and help given to nurture faith in awaiting the coming Redeemer. This does not mean, of course, that the Old Covenant with its healing privileges was superior to the New Covenant. It was rather an accommodation of God's grace to the inferiority of the Old Covenant. Tangible physical blessing was promised in view of the absence of the greater spiritual blessings to come under the New Covenant.

How does God heal today?

Obviously, God heals through natural means and also

through faith and prayer. He does heal, but not always, because it is not always his will to do so. God is completely free to heal or not to heal, according to his will (cf. John 5: 13-16). He may want to use physical infirmity and sickness to test, strengthen, refine, or chasten his people (1 Corinthians 11:30, 31; 2 Corinthians 12:7-10). Even the godliest Christian may be tested in this way.

As a young pastor in Buffalo, New York, from 1934-1940, I had the opportunity to observe firsthand how unbalanced views of faith healing can cause anguish and bondage. A pastor friend in the city was continually exhausting himself, his elders, and his colleagues in unsuccessful attempts to heal the sick through the prayer of faith and anointing with oil as he laid hands upon them. It never occurred to this servant of the Lord that it might not be God's will to grant healing. He was convinced that God would heal all of his people till they reached the age of seventy (Psalms 90:10).

These sincere but misguided notions produced unnecessary bondage and suffering. His own large family suffered because he did not believe in natural means of healing, ruling out doctors and medicines. His wife died in the prime of life. His limited understanding of God's infinite wisdom and mysterious ways plunged his followers in a state of frustrating confusion. Had this dear man of God realized that "the prayer of faith" is divinely given and answered in accordance to God's will, he would have saved himself and his followers a great deal of suffering.

Another example of unbalanced views on divine healing and the resulting anguish was brought to my attention during my student days. A wealthy, elderly maiden lady heard me give a testimony in Baltimore concerning the Lord's healing in my life and offered to assist me financially to attend a certain Christian school. She was in Baltimore because she had undergone a serious but successful operation at the Johns Hopkins Hospital. Earlier in life, this dear Christian woman had been miraculously healed by the Lord in answer to prayer and faith. As a result, she became fanatically opposed to doctors and medicine.

She believed so strongly that faith in God is abrogated by recourse to natural means of healing that she persuaded the board of her church to deny membership to medical doctors. When she finally had to submit to a surgical operation to escape death, she realized how unbalanced and unscriptural her views on healing had been.

Healing as a spiritual gift

The gift as exercised today. Listed among the nine gifts of the Spirit, all of which were given to and employed by the early apostolic Church (1 Corinthians 12:7-11), are "gifts of healing," (literal Greek, "gifts of healings"). Certain of the gifts of the Spirit (1 Corinthians 13:8) which were essential as media of direct inspirational revelation before the New Testament Scriptures were written and circulated for use in the churches (1 Corinthians 13:9, 10) are declared to have been temporary and confined to the apostolic era, but no such declaration is made concerning healing gifts. Such endowments of the Holy Spirit upon certain believers granting them facility and efficacy in praying for the sick were meant to continue in use throughout the Church age and to be in use today.

Since healing must always consider the will of God in each individual case, he who possesses the gifts of healing should ask for discernment (1 Corinthians 12:10). It is not enough to have the necessary faith to pray for the sick. One must be willing to discern and abide by God's will in each case and pray according to the will of God, who knows what is best for us.

The danger of misusing gifts of healing. The mistake of so many who practice faith healing today is to attempt to pray "the prayer of faith" apart from ascertaining God's will in each case. For various reasons, God may choose not to heal the sick believer. The Word of God clearly teaches that God sometimes uses human infirmities and sicknesses to glorify himself and advance believers toward maturity. The faith healer and his followers who rely on their own faith for success are dishonoring God and exposing themselves to possible frustration and despair. There is danger of idolizing God's servant and of prizing physical health above spiritual health, a direct transgression of God's first commandment (cf. Exodus 20:3-5).

More perilous, the demand by the faith healer for healing constitutes an opening to demonic spirits to introduce Satan's program that apes and opposes God. The unwary or poorly taught man of God thus may fall a prey to demonic forces and slip inadvertently into the technique of white magic. Here the religious trappings of unsound doctrine form a mask under which evil spirits may work to effect healings. But these spurious healings require a compensation — a psychic disturbance in exchange for a physical cure, a delusion by a false doctrine and involvement in a cult in exchange for physical relief, or enslavement to some bondage of conscience that tends to fanaticism.

The blessedness of wisely used gifts of healing. When rightly used, gifts of healing produce one of life's greatest blessings. Healing of the believer's body is divinely designed to crown confession of sin and honor the life dedicated to the Lord. Hence the pastor or layman endowed with the gifts of healing ought to be intimately acquainted with the ailing believer in order to ascertain the will of God in each case. This is one reason why James directs the physically sick believer to call for the elders of the church (James 5:14, 15). This puts the responsibility of ascertaining God's will upon the believer who is ill and also upon the elders who are called to pray for him.

The proper situation for praying for the sick, therefore, is not in a public healing campaign where the faith healer knows little or nothing of those who seek his help, but in the privacy and fellowship of a local church.

Observance of this directive would rule out the commercialism and high-pressure methods of healing campaigns which have sensationalized the gospel, disillusioned many seekers, and tarnished the reputation of faith healers.

Scripturally administered divine healing releases the Christian from grievous impediments and also releases the life of Christ and the dynamic of the Holy Spirit in the healthy body of the believer (Romans 8:11). A strong and Spirit-filled saint is prepared to fulfill a triumphant ministry for God. Examples fill the annals of Church history.

The remarkable healing and subsequent ministry of A. B. Simpson, founder of the Christian and Missionary Alliance, offers an illustration of how God can not only deliver his trusting child from weakness and infirmity but abundantly fill his being with the resurrection life of Christ, enabling his healed servant to fulfill great labors and accomplish exploits for God's glory.[2] The Lord waits to touch the weak bodies of his redeemed ones and quicken them to fulfill all his purpose for them in this life.[3]

Healing and the atonement

Is physical healing in the atonement? Did Christ die for the ills of the body as he died for the sins of the soul? The answer must be "No," because the body, although redeemed, remains subject to sin, infirmity, sickness, pain, and death. These physical impediments will not be entirely removed until the redeemed mortal body is glorified at the resurrection or the coming of our Lord. Only spiritual healing, guaranteeing a future glorified body, is in the atonement (Job 19:26; Ephesians 1:14; 4:30; 1 Corinthians 15:53-55).

Healing in the case of a Christian is a direct and sovereign act of God's gracious power, flowing from the cross of Christ, as are all God's blessings to fallen man. It is not an integral part of the atonement and is subject to the will of an all-wise heavenly Father.

This is the reason why, according to Matthew, Isaiah's prophecy that Christ would bear "sicknesses" and carry our "sorrows" (Isaiah 53:4) was fulfilled in Christ's ministry of physical healing (Matthew 8:17), not in his atoning death on the cross. Christ's miracles of healing served to certify him as the Redeemer and were signs of the spiritual healing he came to bring. At the same time they were pledges of the ultimate full deliverance of the redeemed, not only from sin, but from every evil consequence of it in the body as well as in the soul. In this sense only did Christ atone for our physical sicknesses.

Is it always God's will to heal a believer? Advocates of healing in the atonement say, "Yes" and insist that it is never the divine will for a believer who is in the right relationship with God to remain sick.[4] But since this claim is made on the unsound premise that physical healing is in the atonement, it is not borne out by Scripture nor the experience of many Spirit-led believers who have had to cope with physical infirmity and even deformity all their lives. They were not able to pray "the prayer of faith" (James 5:14-16) because it was not God's will for them to be healed and he did not grant them such faith. Genuine physical healing is not given unless it is according to God's will.

When God has guided and enabled men to pray the "prayer of faith," the resulting miraculous cure was not the bequest of Christ from the cross offered to all believers but claimed by only a few.[5] Rather, it was a direct and sovereign act of God's gracious power released according to his special plan for individual believers redeemed by the cross.

Healing by demonic power

The danger of delusion. Seekers after supernatural cures may be deluded into a healing by demonic power. The distinction between divine miracle and demon-energized magic can sometimes be detected only by biblically knowledgeable Christians and possessors of the gift of discerning spirits (1 Corinthians 12:10).

The danger of delusion increases in these last days as demonic activity accelerates and serious study of God's Word wanes. It is a patent fact that sound Bible teaching often is lacking in circles that highlight miracles and healings and gifts of the Spirit. Sometimes the so-called "distinctive truths" are mere doctrinal hobbies and perversions of the Word of God. When these focus on anything other than Jesus Christ and the full scriptural revelation, counterfeit powers of demons may infiltrate lives.

This warning is desperately needed by God's born-again people (1 John 4:1). Present-day Christians must recognize that the Bible, rightly understood and implicitly obeyed, is the only sure protection against demonic delusion and despoilment. Evil powers can accomplish their deceptions only when the Word of God is ignored or disdained —and many Christians are susceptible to demonic influence today because they have ignored God's revelation in his Word. The Bible is impregnable armor for the Christian — when he lives in it!

Obviously, a conjurer who invokes God's name and deceptively forces a cure with the alleged help of God opposes or disregards God. "Theologically viewed, such a venture is basic rebellion. Man commands the transcendent authority. Man wants to have God at his disposal. This arrogance is the basic position of magic."[6]

The dynamic of white magic. Demonic powers energize the practice of white magic, inasmuch as it opposes God and his will. This can happen even when the Scriptures are professedly followed, with "Christian" prayers, laying on of hands, and anointing with oil, though without magic rigmarole and enchantment procedures. If the practice opposes God's will as expressed in Scripture, danger of demonic intrusion is present.

In some European countries where magic conjuration and occultism in general have been cultivated and followed for many centuries, the method of conjuring is very complex and tainted with superstition. The name of the triune God is used in enchantment which aims to place the divine powers in the service of man. Charm words are often underscored by charm acts, such as stroking or sprinkling with the ashes of a burned reptile or with water drawn from a pond at midnight at Easter, etc. The transference conjuration aims at banning the sickness by sending it into some animal or inanimate object. Often amulets inscribed with Scripture are used.

Magic literature reputedly guides the healing conjurer in subjecting the spirit-helper. The purpose is to force a cure, allegedly with the help of God, but the enlisted spirits are not of

God. The popular manual on magic, *The Sixth and Seventh Books of Moses,* instructs the would-be healer in enlisting the help of evil spirit-powers.

The objects of healing conjurations are usually sick humans, but in certain parts of Europe, as the Black Forest of Germany, conjuring of cattle is also common. Many farmers feel conjuring is cheaper and produces quicker results than the services of a veterinarian. Conjuring fruit trees, supposedly to make them more productive, is also practiced.

The deceptiveness of healing by white magic. Since cures by white magic take place under the guise of Christian truth and allegedly by the power of God, this type of healing is much more widespread than black magic and much more deceptive. Naïve believers, and sometimes those who have some knowledge of God's Word, are ensnared, believing this healing method to be Christian.

In reality the use of the Lord's name to effect such healings violates the second commandment of the Decalogue. "Thou shalt not take the name of the Lord thy God in vain, for the Lord will not hold him guiltless that taketh his name in vain" (Exodus 20:7). The Hebrew reads literally, "who takes up (lifts up) his name for falsehood," i.e., uses it in wickedness to deceive or to give a wrong impression. This is exactly what the magic healer does. He prostitutes God's holy name for an unworthy purpose. God is not a handyman who obeys when the magic charmer commands.

Nor can God be used as a tool and be forced by man, even unconsciously and ignorantly. The use of force in prayer is completely at variance with simple trust and obedience inculcated throughout God's Word, and runs counter to the believer's petition, "Thy will be done in earth, as it is in heaven" (Matthew 6:10).

Pressure in prayer can never be justified, not even on the assumption that physical healing is in the atonement as an immediate blessing and can be claimed in God's will by every believer. Believing that all illness is of the devil[7] cannot keep the faith healer from falling into the magic and the demonic, or, at best, into the sphere of mental suggestions, where cures may also be effected.[8] This can happen no matter how sincere or godly the practitioner may be.

Evaluating healing ministries in the light of God's Word. Many fine faith healers whose ministry includes genuine healings by God's power are not noted for their theological exactness. For instance, Dr. Charles Cullis, a godly physician of Boston, one of the first faith healers in the United States, did not formulate any system of doctrine regarding the truth he featured in his ministry.

Numerous faith healers have held unsound views on the person and work of the Holy Spirit and on the subject of spiritual gifts and sanctification. Unsound doctrine and erratic practices have been associated with public faith healers to such an extent that the truth of divine healing as taught in the Word of God has been brought into disrepute and neglected by large sections of the Church.

Kurt Trampler, a Munich author and lawyer whose cures have been authenticated by the Freiburg Institute for Parapsychology,[9] uses the name of God and Christ but forsakes the clear line of New Testament teaching, presenting a dangerous mixture of pantheistic, mystic, natural-religious, and Christian elements.[10] The same doctrinal confusion characterizes the ideas and methods of the early American healer, Phinehas Parkhurst Quimby (1802-1866), and the New Thought movement he started. All sin and sickness were considered an illusion of the mind. Just as a person under hypnosis can think away his pain, so, it was taught, can anyone in the waking state. By considering pain and sickness and their causes as illusions you may make them disappear.[11]

This essentially antichristian idea became a basic concept of Mary Baker Eddy (1821-1910).[12] Healed under Quimby, Mrs. Eddy subsequently became the founder of the cult called Christian Science. It promotes the idea of healing by mind over matter, a kind of mental therapy in which the supernatural is said to operate. This system blatantly distorts God's Word and is basically antichristian.[13]

Faith healers whose teachings and methods are tinged with magic and superstition need to be examined for possible occult subjection. In view of the fact that occult powers and subjection can be passed down through as many as four generations,[14] and psychic abilities persist even after God regenerates a soul, Christian people should be careful not to mistake white magic for genuine miracles by the Holy Spirit.

Kurt Koch has carefully researched the background of the American faith healer William Branham and maintains that he inherited occult subjection from his parents, who believed in fortune-tellers. Koch maintains that Branham exhibits animal-magnetism, mesmerizing, clairvoyance, and magic elements in addition to biblical attributes.[15] Of course, Christ can free the new believer from all occult powers. But caution should always be exercised since Satan can parade as an angel of light.

Evaluating actual healings in the light of God's Word. Miraculous healings can be interpreted as either divine or demonic. Christ healed by divine power and handed the gift on to his disciples. There is no reason to believe that such "gifts of healing" (1 Corinthians 12:9) have been withdrawn from the Church, as were some other apostolic bestowments (1 Corinthians 13:8). "But there are also demonic powers which do not exist just in the imagination of frightened men. They also can work miracles."[16]

The world in which the early Christians lived was full of demons and demon-energized healers and magic workers (cf. Acts 8:9-11; 13:7-10). In the temple of Serapis at Alexandria, Egypt, multitudes of pagans were remarkably healed. Pilgrimages to Epidaurus in Greece became world famous, and a night's sleep in the sacred temple cured thousands. Appolonius of Tyana (3 B.C. — A.D. 96) was a well-known miracle worker who effected magic cures and was regarded by many as "a heathen Christ."[17] People almost worshiped him as a god. As Paul Bauer observes: "There must have been at that time an overstrained psychic tension and activities similar to those which take place today in gatherings for healing."[18]

Throughout the Christian era, miracles of physical healing, either by divine or demonic power, have occurred within the professing Christian church and outside it, in both Roman Catholic and Protestant circles. Unusual healings in the Roman Church have given rise to famous centers of pilgrimage throughout the world. Famous among these are Lourdes in southeastern France, Fatima in Portugal, and Konnersreuth in Oberpfalz, Bavaria. Lourdes and Fatima became a mecca for countless pilgrims because of alleged appearances of the Virgin Mary. Konnersreuth was allegedly honored by the appearance of St. Theresa.

At Lourdes, in 1858, the Virgin was claimed to have appeared to 14-year-old Bernadette Soubirous, under the name of the "Immaculate Conception." Interestingly enough, this occurred four years after the papal court had promulgated the unscriptural dogma that Mary, the mother of Jesus, was herself sinlessly conceived. Near Fatima on May 13, 1917, the Virgin supposedly appeared to three children, aged ten, nine, and seven. The children were said to have talked for at least ten minutes with the apparition. Other visions followed and people began to flock to the spot in a ferment of superstitious frenzy, and miracles of healing and other wonders were claimed.

At Konnersreuth a young woman named Theresa Neumann (1898-1962), who had suffered a serious spinal injury with resultant loss of sight, was suddenly cured of her blindness on April 29, 1923, the day Theresa of Liseauz was being beatified. On May 17, 1925, she was suddenly cured of her spinal trouble. She believed that Saint Theresa had appeared and spoken to her. In 1926 the marks of Christ's wounds are claimed to have appeared in her body, from which blood flowed every Friday. Theresa also claimed that she went through the whole experience of Good Friday and heard Jesus and the apostles conversing in Aramaic. She gave many evidences of clairvoyance and telepathy, and allegedly healed a few people by taking their diseases on herself.[19]

In evaluating such miracles of healing it is difficult for Bible believers to see more than the operation of mind over matter and possibly the working of "spirits not of God" (1 John 4:1, 2). However, a loving God does not confine his gracious gifts to those who have the right theology. He looks at the heart and sees what our eyes cannot see. No doubt at Lourdes, Fatima, and Konnersreuth, his favor to the sick can be attributed to his infinite compassion and wisdom.

Spiritism and physical healing. Cures wrought by spiritistic mediums who operate through the séance[20] and fortune-telling belong to the realm of white magic because Christian camouflage and the names of God and Christ are used as fetishes. While spiritism deals more directly with clairvoyance and fortune-telling, it overlaps other demonic phenomena, such as magic. Spiritistic mediums are often healing mediums, and many people have been led to practice spiritism after gaining physical healing.

Satan knows how gullible we all may be. He is willing and able to perform diabolic miracles to deceive men. Satanic healings, as we have seen, merely shift the physical disorder into the psychic plane by bringing the "healed" person into some type of occult bondage.

No one can become involved in spiritism without serious psychic repercussions. Often the healing conjurer is an adept spiritistic medium as well. I have counseled with several Christians who became psychically vexed by dabbling in magic healings and spiritistic séances. One woman became tormented by "poltergeist phenomena" (hearing voices and noises) after consulting a fortune-telling medium. Cases of psychic bondage abound in some areas of Germany and Switzerland among those who consult healing charmers and clairvoyants. The resulting psychic bondage is frequently worse than the physical malady which was supposedly "cured."[21]

Healing by black magic

Black-magic cures versus white-magic cures. That black- and white-magic cures are essentially the same appears from several considerations. 1. They have similar psychic consequences. In both, the principle of compensation prevails.[22] Satan "heals" but demands some sort of payment in the form of psychic enslavement, cult involvement, or bondage to some form of fanaticism. 2. They have similar theological repercussions. Although one has a Christian camouflage and employs a deceptive religious dress, while the other openly subscribes to Satan and demons, neither resorts to God. Evidently the healer (magic conjurer) who wants to force a cure, whether by appealing to God or the devil, is using supernatural powers to further his own ends.

Magic guidebooks, in fact, instruct the occultist in the art of enlisting the spirit agent and so using the transcendent power. Viewed from a biblical perspective, this is basic rebellion of the satanic variety, aiming to have God at one's disposal. Such willful arrogance is the basis of magic, as the student of the Word of God will easily recognize.

Cures by black magic. Black-magic conjuration openly uses the name of Satan and demonic powers. It does not have the deceptive veneer of Christian respectability that white magic adopts. Jannes and Jambres, the magicians of Egypt (Genesis 41:8, Exodus 7:11; 8:7, 18, 19; 2 Timothy 3:8) are examples of men who were adept in the black arts and workers of diabolic miracles. Such occultists were popular in the courts of ancient pagan kings. They not only advised the heads of government but performed supernatural feats, including magical charming of the sick.

The ability of such magicians is conditioned on the human plane by their inherent psychic power, and on the supernatural plane by their degree of abandonment to demonic domination. The effectiveness of a Christian, too, is subject to his native endowments and his willingness to respond to the Holy Spirit and become dynamically useful to the glory of God.

Black magicians, like spiritistic mediums, differ in strength and psychic ability to perform magical feats (satanic miracles). Strong magicians usually owe their success to innate psychic powers. Very frequently they come from a family where the occult arts have flourished for generations. Their innate and inherited occult powers are frequently cultivated and enhanced by the study of magical literature, notably the so-called *Sixth and Seventh Books of Moses.*

To enlist the help of Satan and demons, a pact is often made with the powers of evil, which is a satanic counterpart of dedication to God's will. The subject consciously and willingly gives himself over to Satan and demonic agencies who will help him perform healing conjurations and other supernatural feats. Ordinarily the body is cut and the compact with the devil is written and signed in one's own blood.[23]

After this wicked practice, the power to inflict sickness is normally coupled with the ability to cure sickness, often to seek revenge as a part of persecution and defense magic. Black magicians can inflict sickness on enemies and even cause their death. They are able to bring sickness upon the cattle of an enemy as well.[24] Persecution and defense magic show their satanic character in the intense hatred they generate.

Such phenomena of black magic, however, flourish only when magic literature is diligently studied and its directions carefully followed. This is especially evident in Europe where occult literature has a wide circulation. This "Bible" of occultism outlines the magic procedures for healing and causing disease, showing the student how to use demonic powers to perform supernatural feats. The experiences of those who use this book form a tragic tale of psychic bondage and demonic enslavement.[25]

The counseling cases of Kurt Koch yield the following example of healing by black magic. A twenty-year-old woman was left with one limb shortened as the result of an attack of polio. Released from the hospital as incurable, the girl and her mother were extremely depressed. They resolved to seek the aid of a man who practiced black magic. A substantial sum was first required to purchase a mandrake root resembling a human being, which was to be nursed like an infant by the patient, according to the magician's strict instructions.

After this preliminary treatment the magician had the girl pray psalms of vengeance, which she had to copy, lay under her pillow, and sleep on. During the next phase of treatment the girl had to put two knives under her pillow and stick two other knives into the wall at the head of her bed. In the course of this bizarre therapy, the girl's shortened limb lengthened.

However, after the leg had been healed, the patient developed serious psychic disturbances. She went to her pastor who was completely helpless in this case. The woman could no longer read the Bible or pray. When she attempted to do so, she became filled with blasphemous thoughts. Fearing for her sanity, she gave the mandrake root and an amulet she had received from the magician to her pastor. From then on she lived in mortal fear of revenge from the magician. The leg, which had stretched to normal length during the magical treatment, returned to its shortened condition.[26]

Cases of healing by black magic abound, as well as instances of infliction of diseases. In large sections of American society such phenomena are practically unknown or are looked upon as pure folklore and superstition. This is because magical literature and occult practices in their cruder and more diabolical forms have not invaded the American scene as they have rural Europe. European young men have been known to ask a magic charmer to inflict upon them some disease or disability to make them unfit for military duty![27]

Black magic and fetishism. A fetish is an object magically charged with protective powers against sickness and other ills and calamities. It is basically a charm, sometimes called an amulet, talisman, or good-luck symbol. Superstitious and occultly involved people believe that a fetish, amulet, or protective talisman becomes more effective when suitably inscribed by magic formulas. As fetishism relies upon such magically charged objects for protection, it has its roots in demon-energized idolatry and paganism.

Fetishism is much more than a manifestation of ancient primitive heathenism. It points to the current widespread superstition evidenced by symbols of ill-omen, such as the raven, the black cat, old wives, and the number thirteen. Good-luck charms such as the Christian cross, the Madonna, four-leaf clovers, mascots, etc., where used as fetishes contaminate Christianity with magic.

The problem of fetishism is often closely related to healing or warding off disease. It becomes more serious when belief in the fetish is strengthened by an enchanting pact. Such amulet pacts are often related to the blood pacts of black magic. Sick persons have been known to return to normal as soon as a charm is removed from their person.

A mother who had a twelve-year-old ill daughter is a case in point. All medical treatment had failed. Finally she turned to a pastor who noticed a little chain about the girl's neck, bearing an amulet. At first the mother refused to remove the amulet from her daughter's neck, for she had been strongly advised never to do so. The pastor, well-versed in magic problems, insisted and finally obtained the little case. In it he found an inscribed pact-charm, which he read to the astounded mother and then destroyed. From that day on, the girl's health improved and soon she was able to leave the hospital fully restored.[28]

Physical healings and other supernatural feats performed through black magic are well known in the history of occultism. Countless cases of both healing and infliction of disease stand fully authenticated in antiquity, the Middle Ages, and modern times.[29] Black and white magic with their physical healings and delusive miracles represent the intrusion of demonic deception where God's Spirit alone should operate.

NOTES
CHAPTER 7

1. "Divine healing" is the better term, if it is God who heals, and faith must be in him alone for such healing.
2. For Dr. Simpson's own testimony see A. B. Simpson, *The Gospel of Healing,* pp. 155-174.
3. Cf. Kenneth MacKenzie, *Our Physical Heritage in Christ,* pp. 47-70.
4. So T. J. McCrossan contends that many true saints are not healed because they pray with the proviso, "If it be thy will" (*Bodily Healing and the Atonement,* pp. 91-100).
5. See Simpson, pp. 79, 80; McCrossan, pp. 1-89; MacKenzie, p. 27.
6. Kurt E. Koch, *Christian Counseling and Occultism,* p. 113. For numerous instances of healing by white magic see Koch, *Between Christ and Satan,* pp. 78-84, 91-97.
7. An example of this is the celebrated faith healer and apostle of the modern faith healing movement, John Alexander Dowie (1847-1907). He viewed all sickness as the work of the devil and contended that disease, root and branch, must be eradicated or faith is a dead failure. He violently arraigned against "doctors, drugs, and devils" (MacKenzie, pp. 20-24, 27). *Encyclopaedia Britannica,* 7 (1964): 616.

8. Regarding the psychology of healing, E. L. House declares: "Many schools which practice healing are dangerous. They may be absolutely out of harmony with the New Testament teaching, and yet may heal through the power of suggestion. And because they do heal, many good yet thoughtless people who are healed accept the religion of such schools as true and God-approved" (*The Psychology of Orthodoxy*, pp. 36-41). Cf. MacKenzie, p. 67.

9. Paul Bauer, *Wizards That Peep and Mutter*, p. 83.

10. Koch, *Between Christ and Satan*, pp. 190, 191.

11. Cf. Bauer, p. 78.

12. *Encyclopaedia Britannica*, 7 (1964): 962. Cf. Charles Borden Soloman, "Christian Science," *Encyclopaedia Britannica*, 5 (1964): 700, 701.

13. Cf. William C. Irvine, *Heresies Exposed*, p. 70; Charles S. Braden, *Christian Science Today*.

14. Exodus 20:3-5; cf. Koch, *Christian Counseling*, pp. 153-162.

15. Koch, *Between Christ and Satan*, pp. 193-195.

16. Bauer, p. 85.

17. Albert Henry Newman, *A Manual of Church History*, 1: 32, 161.

18. *Ibid.*, p. 86.

19. Bauer, pp. 92-94. Cf. "Lourdes," *Encyclopaedia Britannica*, 14 (1964): 434; "Fatima," 9 (1964): 115.

20. Says Raphael Gasson, the former spiritistic medium converted to Christ: "There are many spiritualists today who are endowed with this remarkable gift by the power of Satan; and I myself, having been used in this way, can testify to having witnessed miraculous healing taking place at 'healing meetings' in spiritualism" (*The Challenging Counterfeit*, p. 61). See discussion of spiritistic healing, Gasson, pp. 61-65.

21. Cf. Koch, *Christian Counseling*, p. 160, example 105; p. 161, example 113. Cf. W. H. D. Adams, *Witch, Warlock, and Magician*.

22. Koch, *Between Christ and Satan*, pp. 113, 114, 198.

23. For examples of this nefarious practice see Koch, *Christian Counseling*, pp. 127-130. Cf. M. A. Morray, *Witch-cult in Western Europe*.

24. For an amazing example of "pig-killing" magic see Koch, *Between Christ and Satan*, pp. 174-178. Cf. N. Remy, *Demonolatry*.

25. For an account of this evil work and of the trail of woe that has followed its use, see Koch, *Between Christ and Satan*, pp. 167-182. Cf. M. Sommers, *History of Witchcraft and Demonology*.

26. Koch, *Between Christ and Satan*, pp. 89-91. For further discussion of magical charming and cases of healing by black magic, see Koch, *Christian Counseling*, pp. 104-118. Cf. also E. B. Tylor, *Primitive Culture*, 6th ed.; R. R. Marett, *Threshold of Religion;* R. H. Lowie, *Primitive Religion;* H. Williams, *Superstitions of Witchcraft;* J. W. Wickwar, *Witchcraft and the Black Art*.

27. Koch, *Between Christ and Satan*, p. 99.

28. Koch, *Christian Counseling*, p. 133.

29. Cf. Lynn Thorndike, *A History of Magic and Experimental Science*, vols. 1-4; J. G. Frazer, *The Golden Bough*, vols. 1-2, and *The Magic Art*, 3rd ed. (1911); abridged ed., 1925.

Demons and False Religions

One of the most subtle roles of demons is the perverting of revealed truth. They never cease in their endeavor to turn men away from the gospel of Christ and to deny and distort the Word of God. Their activity started when Satan tempted and triumphed over man in Eden. There Satan used a threefold strategy of opposition to God (Isaiah 14:12-14), confirmed falsehood (Genesis 3:4), and slander of the divine goodness (Genesis 3:5; cf. John 8:44). Down through the centuries Satan and his host of demon helpers, who make his presence and power practically ubiquitous, have used the same strategy to tempt men.

When man succumbed to Satan's blandishments, he lost his Edenic innocence and his fellowship with God (Genesis 3:8) and fell under the control of evil spiritual powers, who encourage fallen man to rebel against God's Word and will. As God began to work in redemption (Genesis 3:9-15, 21; cf. John 5:17; 9:4; 17:4), Satan's spiritual hosts waged a persistent and endless counter-campaign to keep man ignorant of divinely revealed truth and redemptive grace in Christ. Satanic strategy always aims to deceive men to the greatest degree possible.

If "the god of this world" cannot totally blind the unbeliever's mind and thus completely hide the gospel from him (2 Corinthians 4:4), he will seduce the believer to the best of his ability. To keep the believer from the simplicity and purity of the gospel of grace, he will encourage all sorts of errors. This is Satan's attempt to retain some degree of control over those who come to a saving knowledge of Christ. Doctrinal error obscures revelation and gives Satan and demonic forces a toehold. Evil powers can confuse man in his attempt to interpret truth, but they cannot penetrate the sure defense of God's infallible Word. The Holy Bible, God's revealed Word, points us to Christ's victory over Satan at the cross. He alone can deliver us from evil and from the evil one.

Demonism and pagan religion

The dynamic of pagan religion. Religion in its broadest sense may be defined as "the belief in spiritual beings."[1] Sir J. G. Frazer defines it as "a propitiation or conciliation of powers superior to man, which are believed to direct and control the course of nature and of human life."[2] By "powers" Frazer means "conscious or personal agents."[3]

According to Scripture, there are both unfallen and fallen "powers." Unfallen powers belong to the realm of good supernaturalism, presided over by the one true God who is Creator of all and Redeemer of mankind. Fallen powers belong to the sphere of evil supernaturalism, presided over by Satan, the first creature of God who fell and introduced sin into a previously sinless universe (Isaiah 14:12-17; Ezekiel 28:11-19; Job 38:6, 7).

The holy, omnipotent, sovereign God governs myriads of elect, unfallen angels and redeemed men. Satan rules myriads of fallen angels or demons, who rebelled against God and who seek to dominate men and enlist them in revolt against the Creator. Pagan religion is an easy prey of evil supernaturalism. Demonic powers constitute the dynamic of heathenism, which represents the first and greatest apostasy (1 Corinthians 10:20; cf. Genesis 3:1-14; Romans 1:21-32).

Divinely revealed truth implies that religion began in monotheism (Romans 1:19-21) and that a turn to primitive demon worship and later to polytheism was the deceptive work of Satan and fallen spirits (1 Timothy 4:1, 2; 1 John 4:1-6; Revelation 9:20, 21). To declare that "the hypothesis of a primitive monotheism lacks foundation, and is intrinsically impossible"[4] is to disregard witness of Holy Scripture. The contention that "monotheism is a late phenomenon of religion"[5] is true only in the sense that Abraham in about 2,000 B.C. was called out of universal polytheism — into which mankind had fallen by that time — to be a witness through his descendants to the knowledge of the one true God (Genesis 12:1-3). This purge from polytheism was necessitated by a long apostasy from an original monotheism.

The truth that the human race began with a monotheistic faith is an inescapable corollary of the fact that man is a direct creation of God and not the product of naturalistic evolution. The theory that man evolved instead of being created contradicts the Word of God so flagrantly that it might well be called a "doctrine of demons."

Unfallen man, fresh from the Creator's hand, enjoyed an ecstatic, monotheistic faith and fellowship. This knowledge and blissful communion with the one true God and Creator were marred by man's succumbing to Satan's deception and power. But sinful man could still approach the infinitely holy God through blood sacrifice. Such sacrifice clearly showed that man was a lost sinner before God until salvation through the Redeemer to come (Genesis 3:15) would provide forgiveness for man's guilt.

Satan and his demon-helpers did their utmost to enslave fallen man. Their goal was to blind man to God's goodness, holiness, and grace; to deceive man concerning his sinful and utterly lost condition apart from divine redemption; and to turn him away from faith in the coming Redeemer, as the only way to God, prefigured by animal sacrifice. It started with Cain, who did not understand God's grace and his own unworthiness when he offered the work of his hands as a means of acceptance before God (Genesis 4:1-7).

Rejection of God's grace justifying man through the shedding of blood in favor of human works to secure divine acceptance (cf. Genesis 4:7) was the first "doctrine of demons" (cf. 1 Timothy 4:1). This deception ushered in man's apostasy which led to the flood in Noah's day and then to the confusion of languages at the tower of Babel. By the time of Abraham the human race had lapsed into universal idolatry. God then raised up Abraham to be the representative of justification by faith (Genesis 15:6; Romans 4:3-5, 13-25) in the midst of a sea of paganism that had lost contact with the one true God.

Demonism and primitive religion. Among aboriginals and primitive cultures, religion is closely allied to magic, superstition, and the worship of evil spirits. Religious beliefs and practices in such areas are dominated by spiritism with its multitude of shadowy spirit beings and malevolent demons. Primitive animism holds that material objects possess life and are indwelt by multitudinous spirits. These evil powers are always feared, ceaselessly placated, and slavishly worshiped.[6] Common in such primitive paganism are the cruder and more superstitious forms of demonism practiced by witch doctors, magicians, charmers, sorcerers, clairvoyants, and demon worshipers. Frequently ignorance fosters inhuman cruelties, and the moral law of God appears blotted out from the creature's consciousness.[7]

In primitive belief there is such an interweaving of magic with religion that the two concepts become merged. Demonic powers are largely regarded as causes of natural and physical phenomena. The course of nature is not attributed to the operation of an orderly universe under immutable laws established by the Creator, but to the working of capricious and often vengeful demons. Primitive religion, accordingly, is conditioned by gross ignorance, binding superstition, and enslavement to demonic powers. Such occult bondage constitutes one of the main reasons for the primitive way of life of aboriginals. Not until the Christian gospel sets them free are they truly liberated. Science and communication with other societies, however, tend to emancipate primitive people from paganism's grosser superstitions and practices.

Demonism and polytheism. Primitive religion, with its worship of a multitude of indeterminate spirits, develops into polytheism when a tribal culture is superseded by a national culture with its advance in arts and sciences and enrichment of personal life and interests. The larger and more constant values of a social order based on agriculture and commerce require supernatural beings capable of responding to a wider range of needs. Polytheism is the answer to these religious demands.[8]

Anthropologists and historians regard polytheism as an advance over more primitive forms of paganism. It liberates religion from bondage to purely local associations and replaces the indistinct spirits of older beliefs with supernatural beings possessing more definite character and spheres of activity. These two phases actually represent different types of demonic deception and strategy. A god, as distinguished from a spirit, may be defined as a supernatural being with determinate qualities which embody the values of which men are conscious.[9] The god's representative image or statue, however, is a nonentity, a figment of a superstitious mind blinded by satanic deceit (2 Corinthians 4:4).[10]

Behind the mythical god represented by its idol-image is the demonic host. The same demons that are worshiped in primitive paganism now hide behind the revered gods and goddesses of more sophisticated and cultured paganism. The subtle allurement of idolatry and the fanatical zeal of its devotees can be explained only on the thesis of revealed truth that "behind the idol there are terrible spiritual presences — demons."[11]

The Apostle Paul, writing to the Corinthians, clearly states: "Observe those physically the people of Israel! Are not those who eat the sacrifice sharers of the altar? What then is my suggestion? That an idol offering amounts to anything, or that the idol itself is anything? No, but that what they sacrifice, they are offering to demons and not to God, and I do not want you to fellowship with demons. You cannot drink the Lord's cup and a demon's cup. You cannot participate in the Lord's table and in a demon's table." (1 Corinthians 10:18-21, Berkeley).

Paul points out an important fact. He shows that while it is true in one sense that an idol has no reality, nevertheless, it has a terrible reality in another sense. Heathenism is under Satan's control. As "prince of this world" he and his demons are indeed worshiped by the heathen, either consciously or unconsciously (cf. Deuteronomy 32:17; Leviticus 17:7; 2 Chronicles 11:15; Psalm 106:37; Revelation 19:20).[12]

In the Greek New Testament, "Devil" (*diabolos*, "accuser") is restricted to Satan. The term "demons" (*daimonia*) is applied strictly to Satan's subordinate spirits who aid him in deluding the dupes of idolatry, enslaving them in fear and turning them away from love and loyalty to God (Exodus 20:1-7). For example, the English word "panic" is derived from Pan, the great nature god, whose human form with horns and cloven hoofs gave rise to the superstitious and ferocious portrayals of Satan, and fear is the spirit of Satan and his demons (James 2: 19).[13]

Although the motivating factors of polytheism are complex, and in some cases remarkable men have been elevated to the rank of gods,[14] demonism always remains the dynamic behind the zeal of idolatrous devotees. This fact remains true whether the deity is a national god like the Babylonians' Marduk, the Assyrians' Ashur, the Greeks' Zeus, the Romans' Jupiter, or is a deity of exceedingly varied character like Apollo, or a nature god like the Egyptian sun-god, Ra, or belongs to the hosts of lesser deities.

Demonism and non-Christian religions

A cursory review of the religious situation of the world reveals the powerful hold Satan and demonic powers have upon the fallen human race. In listing the principal religions of the world, the *Britannica Book of the Year 1965*[15] estimated the world population in 1964 at roughly 3.2 billion, with the total Christian population considerably less than one billion. Since this last figure includes almost three-fifth billion Roman Catholics, slightly less than a quarter-billion Protestants, and about one-seventh billion Greek Orthodox, one can readily see that truly born-again believers are a relatively small percentage of the world's population.

Over two billion of the world's population are either religionless or members of faiths that offer no true knowledge of

God and solid spiritual hope. This vast segment of humanity includes Muslims, who are pushing toward the half-billion mark, Hindus and Confucianists (each over a third of a billion), Buddhists (over a quarter of a billion) and Shintoists and Taoists, who together number over one-tenth billion. Others include primitive animists and those with no religion at all (almost three-quarter billion), not to mention between thirteen and fourteen million Jews and almost one-seventh million Zoroastrians. Political communism dominates one billion of these lives and constitutes a sinister tool of Satan.

The origin of false religions

The inspiration of false religions. The false religions of the world, including the perverted cults of Christianity, are all demon-inspired. As the prince of this world, Satan is bent on turning men away from the revealed truth of the one true God and from the salvation he has provided for sinful mankind through his Son, Jesus Christ. This is clearly taught in the Word of God. The Apostle Paul stresses this fact not only in connection with idolatry (1 Corinthians 10:20), but with all false doctrines, including those of so-called Christian cults.

Since departures from the faith were called "doctrines of demons" by Paul (1 Timothy 4:1-6), it stands to reason that all false religions are demon-inspired. Before pointing to demonism as the source of doctrinal error, the apostle had just summarized the essential verities of the Christian faith (1 Timothy 3:16). The essential truths of Christianity, as expressed here, include: (1) *the incarnation* — "He (God) was manifested in the flesh" (R.S.V.); (2) *Christ's death and resurrection* — "vindicated by the Spirit" (Berkeley); (3) *Christ's divine Person and finished redemptive work attested by the elect, unfallen angelic creation* — "seen by angels"; (4) *the efficacy of Christ's finished redemptive work demonstrated* — "believed on in the world"; (5) *the divine seal set upon Christ's finished redemptive work* — "received up into glory."

This creed setting forth essential Christian truth is incorporated by the apostle to furnish the standard by which all doctrinal error is to be exposed and the false in religious profession and practice identified wherever it is found. Having presented this criterion of truth, Paul proceeds to outline the source of error in demonism (1 Timothy 4:1-6). Here the apostle speaks with the deepest solemnity, almost as if his prophetic utterance by the Holy Spirit were independent of his own participation.

"But the Spirit speaketh expressly" (*hreros legei,* "distinctly asserts") "that in the latter times some shall depart from the faith, giving heed to seducing spirits and doctrines of devils (demons)." The "latter times" include the entire age of the Church, Paul's time as well as ours, but have particular relevance to the age-end apostasy just preceding Christ's coming for his own. At the end of the latter times, demon activity will precipitate the great falling away from the essential core of Christian truth, which Jude calls "the faith once for all delivered to the saints" (Jude 1:3), resulting in the false ecumenism of the apostate church of the end-time (Revelation 17:1-18).

The important point is that those who "fall away from the faith" are said to give "heed to seducing spirits," that is, "deceiving demons." They are the invisible spiritual agents behind the visible human agents or false teachers. Yielding and subscribing to deluding demons results in "doctrines of demons," not to be confused with teachings about demons (demonology).

Such "doctrines of demons" honeycomb man-concocted religions and influence the false cults of Christianity. Those who "yield to deluding spirits and demonic teachings" (Berkeley) do so "through the hypocrisy of those who speak lies, whose own consciences are seared" into insensitivity to truth with the "branding iron" of cherished error. Through the base insincerity and perfidy of false teachers, demonic teachings are taught and promulgated. The false teacher first departs from the truth, next he listens to and cooperates with "deluding spirits." This is how "doctrines of demons" are born.

The apostle, for purpose of illustration, deals with a particular doctrine of demons which was plaguing the young pastor, Timothy, in his parish. This was a type of legalistic asceticism, in this case forbidding marriage and enjoining abstinence from certain kinds of food (1 Timothy 4:3-5), an error common in Christianity and also in non-Christian religions. Doctrines of demons are multifarious in form and almost endless in variety. They appear in manifold perversions of pure Christianity within the Babel of cults parading under the banner of the Church and as spiritual monstrosities within the benighted religions of the world.

The propagating power of false religions. The fanatical zeal of the cultist or the false prophet should not be surprising. When demons instigate errors, they take endless pains to propagate them. As Van Baalen aptly notes: "Cultists are not people who have to be aroused to an interest in religion."[16] Satan and his demon-helpers have always had an interest in religion and are themselves essentially religious. But theirs is a religion of pride, self-ambition, God-opposition, and deception. People who feel that all religions are good and who are unable to "discern spirits" (1 Corinthians 12:10) are ready prospects for demonic deception.

The Apostle John presents the revelation that demonism is the impelling power that propagates false doctrine. "Beloved, believe not every spirit, but prove the spirits, whether they are of God, because many false prophets are gone out into the world" (1 John 4:1). A spirit may be believed, rightly or wrongly, when the "prophet" brings a message from the invisible spirit. The real speaker behind the prophet is either the Spirit of God, the omniscient Teacher, or a demon spirit or spirits. "The Spirit of truth" leads into "all truth," and speaks through the true man of God and teacher of sound doctrine (John 16:13). Demonic spirits under Satan, "the spirit of error" (1 John 4:6), speak through the cultist or false religionist to disseminate erroneous doctrine and foster heresy.

God's "beloved" are often extremely naïve about satanic guile, and the Apostle John singles them out for warning, since all such children of God are the special targets of Satan. They are those whom Satan would like to trap in some error, en-

snare in some cult, and saddle with some fanatical view or
flagrant heresy, all in the name of alleged truth and spirituality.

*The acid test to differentiate true religion from false re-
ligion.* The Apostle John urges God's "beloved" not to believe
"every spirit," but to "try the spirits" in the sense of putting
them to the acid test of the Word of God (cf. 1 Corinthians 12:
10). Unless this caution is strictly followed, God's people stand
in peril of being taken in by demon-energized false prophets
who have "gone out into the world" to start Christ-denying
cults.

In the clearest terms, John centers the test in the glorious
Person and finished redemptive work of our Lord Jesus Christ.
"Hereby know ye the Spirit of God" — this is the intent of the
doctrinal test, to recognize the Holy Spirit as the omniscient,
sole, and all-sufficient Revealer of truth, and to recognize his
truth amid the clamor of alien voices energized by "spirits not
of God." These demon spirits speaking through false teachers
pervert or distort to whatever degree they are able the full
truth of who Jesus Christ is and what he accomplished by his
death and resurrection. Only the Holy Spirit can confirm the
reality of Christ's Person and finished redemptive work to a
person and save him from the god of this world.

"Every spirit," that is, every witness who speaks by the inspiration of the Holy Spirit, "confesseth" (freely and readily
recognizes the fact) that "Jesus Christ is come in the flesh."
This involves the confessing of a twofold truth: (1) that Jesus
is the Redeemer of men; (2) "he is come in the flesh"; this
means he was "the Son of the living God" (Matthew 16:16;
John 6:69; Hebrews 1:2, 5; 1 John 4:15), the predicted virgin-born "seed of the woman" (Genesis 3:15), the preincar-
nate Word, who was "with God and was God" (John 1:1), who
became man (John 1:14) — God and man in one Person, Em-
manuel, or God with us (Matthew 1:18-25).

The confession that "Jesus Christ is come" (*ēlēluthōta,*
a perfect "having come," not a mere past historical fact but
present and continuing in its blessed effects) to earth in the
"flesh" also asserts our Lord's real humanity, both his sinless,
unglorified human body before his death and his resurrected

and glorified human body presently at the right hand of the Father. This is the pledge and guarantee that the body of every believer will be glorified as his is (1 John 3:1-3).

Our Lord's "flesh" (true humanity) implies his death for us, for only by God's becoming man could he die (Hebrews 2:9, 16). Moreover, his death implies his love for us (John 15: 13). To deny the reality of Christ's humanity, therefore, is to deny his love. This is what every spirit does who does not acknowledge Jesus in the flesh. Such a spirit "is not from God; it is the spirit of Antichrist of whose coming you have heard. Right now he is in the world" (1 John 3:3, Berkeley).

In this unambiguous manner the Apostle John gives us the acid test for differentiating false religions from the true and the Holy Spirit from demon spirits. Together with the Apostle Paul (1 Timothy 3:16—4:2), the Apostle John gives God's criterion for judging between the true and the false in the complex realm of religions. Deception will surely engulf people who follow man's voice instead of God's and who ride with ecumenical trends that depreciate God's Word and approve false shepherds within the professing church.

Demonism and the great ethnic religions

How should a Christian view other religions? This question is hotly debated in a day of ecumenicity and religious pluralism. Many churchmen insist that truth is not exclusive but is scattered throughout all of humanity and is spoken throughout the culture which first gave it expression. Proponents of pluralism, accordingly, deny truth comes from God to man through a Spirit-given revelation — the Bible. Instead they look for truth which passes from man to man in their dialogue about life. Such a movement represents a determined effort in today's world to throw off the restraint imposed by any truth presented as "the only infallible rule of faith and practice."[17]

It is a common thing in the ecumenical atmosphere of the times to be told that Christian missions is a seeking of truth together with the adherents of non-Christian religions rather than a proclamation of truth which God has supernaturally revealed in the Bible. To hold that the revealed Word of God offers an infallible standard and criterion both for judging non-Christian religions and the cults and isms that parade under the Christian banner is to run the risk of being dubbed a narrow bigot guilty of unscholarly and nonsensical prejudice.[18]

Those who honor the Word of God as fully inspired and authoritative must accept the test it presents to determine what is true and false in religion if they are to avoid the snare of demonic delusion. All who give Christ and God's Word their rightful place of honor will heartily agree with Stuart P. Garver, editor of *Christian Heritage,* who aptly observes: "Pluralism is inadmissible whenever it is at variance with what God has revealed in his Word. As a community of faith, the Christian Church is committed to a Word of which Jesus said, 'Not one jot nor one tittle shall fail.' Whether we like it or not, we must live with that Word. The very idea that God would expect the scientist to reject his theories once they are found to be at variance with the Creator's established order of the universe, but did not provide theologians with any viable, precise, and authoritative data which would infallibly test the accuracy of their teachings is an insult to divine intelligence."[19]

The very limitations of pluralism offer an awesome challenge to the churches. It is quite obvious that fragments of truth are to be found in the prophetic repositories of pluralism. Those whom the apostle called to account for preaching "another gospel" are not said to completely lack truth. But their message is adulterated and laced with errors, violating the essential criterion of the Word concerning the glorious Person and all-sufficiency of the finished redemption of Christ (1 Timothy 3:16; 1 John 2:1, 2).

The false gospels of non-Christian religions, in fact, frequently add doctrines that are as dangerous as what they omit and may well turn the hearers' hearts against Christian truth. "The challenge of pluralism, therefore, is not to compound this mixture of truth with untruth in the gospels of pluralism but to displace the perverted gospel of the world with the pure gospel revealed from heaven by the Spirit of God in the Person of Christ."[20]

What the Christian's attitude toward other religions should be is well summarized by a veteran missionary of another generation. "We do not come to men of other creeds, Hindus, Muslims, Buddhists, seeking to impose upon them a 'Western religion,' but in the spirit of the apostle, 'I have delivered unto you that which I also received, how that Christ died for our sins, that he was buried, and that he rose again the third day, according to the Scriptures!' God sent us this gospel by missionaries from Asia. We have received Christ as our Savior. And now God has sent us back to Asia, with the same gospel, not on some airplane of fancied superiority, boasting our civilization, inventions, or national bigness, but as humble pilgrims vending priceless pearls from celestial seas."[21]

Demonism and Hinduism

Hinduism is the major religion of India, embracing at least ninety percent of its population. This ninety percent constitutes ninety-five percent of the world's adherents to this faith. Nearly all remaining Hindus reside in Pakistan and Ceylon, with small minorities found in Burma, Malaya, South Africa, Fiji, Trinidad, and the territories of British East Africa. The total number of Hindus exceeds 395,000,000.

Hinduism, as it exists today, is a syncretism primarily of Brahmanism and Buddhism, worshiping a multitude of deities who are believed to reside in animate and inanimate objects. Hinduism is actually a way of life whose precepts encompass a vast range of human activity outside the scope of most modern religions. A distinction must be drawn between the orthodox Hindu, who still respects much of his ancient religion, and the modern, educated Indian who calls himself a Hindu but breaks with much of the traditions of the past.[22]

In its traditional form the chief distinguishing features of Hinduism are (1) the doctrine of the reincarnation of souls into other bodies at death; (2) the corollary belief that all

living beings are the same in essence; (3) a complex polytheism, subsumed in a fundamental monotheism by the teaching that all lesser gods are subsidiary aspects of the one God;
(4) a deep-rooted tendency to mysticism and monistic philosophy, holding that there is only one kind of substance or
ultimate (spirit), with every creature seeking emancipation
from further migrations to effect junction with the universal
spirit; (5) a stratified system of social classes (castes); (6)
a syncretistic tendency to assimilate rather than separate and
exclude, in marked contrast to Judaism and Christianity. In
the sacred *Bhagavad Gita,* the incarnate god Krishna says,
"Whatever god a man worships, it is I who answers the
prayer."[23]

Whatever may be said concerning Hinduism, it has no doubt
helped unregenerate man make life in a sin-cursed world
more bearable, otherwise it would not have survived for so
many centuries, ostensibly as a vital spiritual force. But the
power behind it is demonic, as measured by the criteria set
forth in the inspired Word of God. It, of course, rejects the Person of Jesus Christ and the all-sufficiency of his redemptive
work. Hence it offers no personal salvation, no bodily resurrection, no liberation of the spirit for communion with a forgiving
God, no solid hope for heaven.

But can Hinduism give a transcendent experience? Can it
bring one in contact with the realm of the supernatural? Can
it effect life changes? The answer is, of course, that it can and
does, because behind it, as behind all false religions, are
"spirits not of God" (1 John 4:1, 2). These spirits are "evil" in
that they oppose God's will and God's Word, but all of them are
not low, vile, and vicious in manner. Many are refined, even
"kind" and beneficent in a restricted sense. Indeed, many
demons, like Satan, parade as an "angel of light." This explains
in part the babel of cults that parade under the Christian
banner, and why ancient Oriental faiths can invade a so-called
"Christian" America and obtain a foothold.[24]

An example is the cultivation of yoga, one of the branches
of the Hindu philosophy, which teaches the doctrine of the
Supreme Being and explains how the human soul may obtain

emancipation from further migrations and effect union with the universal spirit. The means used for this include a long continuance in unnatural postures, withdrawal of the senses from external objects, concentration of the mind on some grand central truth, and the like. *Life* magazine displays a young man, Tom Law, sitting in the ancient lotus position in the stillness of the mountainous district near Santa Fe, New Mexico, and greeting the dawn with "the breath of fire," a yoga breathing exercise.[25]

Says Tom: "Yoga is a technique for getting yourself high. And being high is to discover that all natural things are spiritual. It's how we all want to feel. Yoga gets me reconnected. As soon as I get into the position it begins to happen to me. The center of the earth becomes located in my stomach, my head is in the stars, and yet I am here too. Yoga really works, which is why I think it will be popular. People are sick of having to take something to get high, first of all, and also it's in the old American tradition of do-it-yourself."[26]

Demonism and Confucianism

Confucianism is the doctrine and system of morality taught by Confucius (551-478 B.C.), China's most famous man, whose ideas have deeply influenced the civilization of eastern Asia. Confucianism inculcates civil, family, and social duties long adopted in China as the basis of education and law. But since it does not worship any god, Confucianism can scarcely be called a religion. In practice, however, it forms one religious compound with Taoism and Buddhism. It supplies the political-moral element, while Taoism furnishes the religious and magical vein, and Buddhism offers the theosophic, or mystical pagan concept of transmigration of souls from one body to another until eventual conjunction with the divine is allegedly attained.

Confucius himself avoided discussion of spirits, demons, and life after death. His emphasis was upon life here and now. He taught people to "respect spirits but keep them at a distance," not because he was irreligious, but because he wanted men to direct their own destiny by sound moral living rather than allow the spirits to do so.[27] His view of immortality was purely humanistic — the immortality of virtue, wisdom, and achievement. Confucianism, therefore, does not predicate heaven and hell as a place and state after death, nor does it have any clear concept of a personal God, whom it approximates, however, by the idea of a spiritual reality called "heaven." This it considers the ground of all principles and the source of the moral law. Confucianism inculcates a naturalistic law of retribution, according to which good and evil deeds will bring their own consequences in this life.

As a system of practical morality rather than a religion, Confucianism does not delve into the realm of the supernatural and is not directly connected with the demonic. Its demonic impress is seen, however, in its omissions (God, salvation in Christ, eternal life, etc.), leaving men without redemption and a reliable hope for eternity. But as far as contributing to the moral and temporal betterment of unregenerate mankind, Confucianism, like all merely humanistic religions, has a limited beneficial ministry.

All men, whether regenerate or unregenerate, will be judged by God according to their deeds in this life. The regenerate are saved solely by faith in God's redemptive grace in Christ (Ephesians 2:8-10), but will be rewarded or will suffer loss of reward at the judgment seat of Christ for their response to God's eternal moral law (2 Corinthians 5:10). The unregenerate, including millions of sincere and "decent" Confucianists, will be judged by the same moral law. Although deprived of heaven, these moralistic religionists will suffer varying degrees of punishment in eternal hell, being judged "according to their works" (Revelation 20:11-15).

Shall a religion of works and morality benefit pagans? Most emphatically, "Yes." Although such a religion producing such a life cannot save them, it can stand them in good stead at the divine judgment of the unregenerate that introduces the eternal state. Although they will never know glorification of the body and a sinless association with Christ in a sin-cleansed universe, they will be accorded the place their lives on earth have merited in the eyes of an infinitely just, loving, and righteous Judge.

Demonism and Buddhism

Buddhism's origin is traced to Gautama Buddha (c. 563-483 B.C.), a prince reared in luxury in northeast India. In his twenty-ninth year, the prince forsook all worldly honor and comfort to seek "supreme peace of Nirvana." This meant deliverance from the painful realities of life's transitoriness, as evidenced by the endless round of birth, old age, sickness and death, repeated according to Indian belief through countless successive rebirths. Failing to achieve his goal by extreme asceticism, Gautama gained great enlightenment by quiet meditation, becoming "Buddha" — "The Enlightened One." He concluded the cause of suffering is a craving due to ignorance, and proclaimed a way for its removal through mental discipline and right living.[28]

Buddhism's stress on mental discipline and right living, like the practical morality of Confucianism, has doubtless enabled millions to live more noble lives and produced varying degrees of natural satisfaction. But such a system of human works cannot provide a way to personal salvation. By following the path of mental discipline and right living, the Buddhist disciple has only a vague hope of being freed from the necessity of rebirth (reincarnation, the soul transmigrating to some other life) and of attaining Nirvana.

Nirvana itself is a delusive dream. Even if "the purified saint" did attain Nirvana, after all the sufferings and disciplines of countless rebirths and reincarnations, this final state is extinction, not glorification. Worse still, Buddhism provides no power to be "purified" in order to become "a saint" who could attain this imagined goal of Nirvana; it provides no Savior nor a realistic conception of sin.

Considered in the light of the revealed Word of God and the glorious Person and redemptive work of Christ, Buddhism is exposed as a system of self-effort and ultimate frustration, unable to regenerate the soul or to bring "life and immortality to light through the gospel" (2 Timothy 1:10). It does not offer good news. As a religion of works, it has kept men in spiritual poverty and is nothing more than a brilliant satanic invention to keep men away from the saving grace of God. It cultivates human virtues and gives an appearance of saintly piety attained by human effort apart from God's help. Since it parades as an angel of light, many have not seen its demonic character.

Considered positively, however, Buddhism, like Confucianism and Hinduism, has helped countless millions of unregenerate men to observe the moral laws of God as they pertain to everyday morality. It has helped to make the lot of millions much more bearable both in this life and in the life to come (eternal hell). It must be remembered that God is just and merciful and will judge every man according to his works, those saved by Christ as well as those lost in non-Christian religions (Revelation 20:11-15).

Demonism and Taoism

Taoism is a religion of China, traditionally founded by Lao-tse in the sixth century B.C.[29] It ranks with Confucianism and Buddhism as one of the three great religions of China.[30] There are even "temples of the three doctrines" where idols of Buddha and Lao-tse flank Confucius. The folk-faith of the Chinese primitive, Taoism features a multiplicity of gods, occultism, and superstitions, including geomancy, fortune-telling, divination, magic, and use of charms. This pronounced occultism also appears in some Buddhist sects, notably in Tibet and Mongolia where demonic phenomena such as spirit-worship, divination, magic, and sorcery abound.[31]

Taoism reflects a wholesale imitation of Buddhism, notably in its temples, clergy, images, ceremonies, canon, and general morality. Since most of its followers also subscribe to Confucianism and Buddhism, the Taoist religion shares their ethical emphasis. Accordingly, it bears the same demonic imprint that the other great non-Christian religions of Asia display. However, it is more deeply connected with idolatry through the overt demonic phenomena characteristic of common folk and peasant classes.

Demonism and Shintoism

Shintoism (Chinese *shin,* "spirit," and *tao,* "way") is one of the principal religions of Japan. Originally, it was a form of nature worship, regarding the forces of nature as deities and the sun as the supreme god. The soul of the sun god, when on earth, reputedly founded the reigning house. Hence the emperor was worshiped as of divine origin until the end of World War II, when the imperial-cult was abolished. The essence of worship is now ancestral veneration and sacrifice to departed heroes.

Like the masses in China, the common people of Japan invoke deities of all sorts, depending upon their needs. Various occult practices such as divination, fortune-telling, spiritism, magic, and conjuring are found and have infiltrated into official Shintoism and Buddhism as well.[32]

Of course, Shintoism offers no way of salvation and is to be evaluated in much the same way as other non-Christian faiths. However, from a temporal aspect, it also has had a beneficial ministry to millions. From the standpoint of the infinitely holy and merciful God, it is totally lacking in bringing man's deepest need to God for forgiveness and acceptance.

Demonism and Islam

Islam is a system of belief and practice established by the Arab prophet Mohammed (A.D. 570?-632). Today at least every seventh human being is a Muslim. An estimated 455 million Moslems form the bulk of the population of Northern Africa and Western Asia, and extend all the way through India into Malaya, Indonesia, and the Philippines. Although Islam is a monotheistic movement, deadly opposed to the idolatrous pagan religions, it bears a strong demonic stamp. This appears in its rigid unitarian concept of God, which denies the deity of Christ and reduces him to a mere human prophet, inferior to Mohammed himself. Indeed, Mohammed is claimed to be "the seal of the prophets" (*Koran* 33:40), the last and therefore the greatest. He is considered the sole channel of revelation for his own time and generation, and the last apostle for all times and all generations.

With the denial of Christ's deity, Islam repudiates God's salvation. Thus this religion was conceived in the spirit of Antichrist (cf. 1 John 4:1-6) and offers no deliverance from sin to its followers. Islam also blatantly denies the Word of God, claiming the *Koran* instead to be the uncreated word of God, dictated piece by piece in Arabic to Mohammed by the angel Gabriel. Despite the fact that Islam believes in a final judgment, immortality of the soul, rewards for the righteous in heaven, and punishment for the wicked in hell, it offers no legitimate way for fallen men to reach heaven.

Islam (Arabic, *islam,* "surrender") means "submission" to the will of God. But even this concept is a demonic delusion, for in rejecting the Person and redemptive work of Christ Islam rejects God's will.[33] Its history of savagery and conquest by the sword in the name of God and truth bears the mark of Satan, "the liar" and "the murderer from the beginning" (John 8:44). No religion is so callous to divinely revealed truth in Christ. No people have displayed clearer evidences of the demonic dynamic and zeal that characterize all promoters of false religions. Muslims distort Old Testament truth as Christian cultists distort New Testament truth.[34]

Demonism and Judaism

As the religion of more than thirteen million Jews throughout the world, Judaism rests principally upon the inspired Hebrew Scriptures of the Old Testament. Judaism is founded on two basic doctrines: (1) monotheism, the belief in the one and only God; (2) the covenant election of the nation Israel to proclaim its faith to the world.[35] Monotheistic beliefs as well as concepts of covenanting gods can be traced to other religions in which the relation between deity and worshipers is usually rooted in natural and physical associations, but in Judaism "it is determined exclusively by an act of free choice whereby God discloses his presence and will to his elect."[36]

As a result, the distinctive features of Judaism are these seven. (1) Divine transcendence. God is unbounded by any manifestation of physical existence. But Judaism, in failing to see Christ as God incarnate and immanent, missed the prophetic meaning of its own Scriptures, thereby forfeiting the Savior and his salvation. This blinding operation of Satan and demons (2 Corinthians 4:4, Romans 11:1-25) produced the tragic spectacle of present-day Jewish confusion and unbelief.

(2) God as ground of all existence. He is sole creator of all things. (3) Ethical conception of God. He is not a mere force but a personality possessing the highest moral qualities. (4) Concern for individual moral culture. Hebrew monotheism not only recognizes the ethical character of God, but calls men to conform to the divine pattern (Leviticus 19:2). (5) Universalism. The one true and holy God becomes the object to be worshiped by all men everywhere. Every creature is bound to honor God and obey his moral law. (6) Election for service. The nation was chosen to make known the one true God to all men. (7) Unity of divine purpose in history. Everywhere else (except in Christianity) history is basically meaningless, a mere repetition of crimes and misery. But the quest of the one true God leads to a realization of God's ultimate purpose in history.[37]

By rejecting Jesus Christ, God incarnate, Judaism temporarily forfeited its high calling and place in God's purpose in history, until the Jews turn to Christ at his second advent (Zechariah 12:10—13:1; Romans 11:25-36). Then their spiritual blindness shall be lifted and they shall be delivered from the demonic delusion that has rested upon them (Matthew 12:43-45) since they recklessly cried, "His blood be on us, and on our children" (Matthew 27:25).[38]

Demonism and cults

It is not surprising to find an appalling display of satanic power and duplicity in places where Christ's redemptive power is not known. Satan's prime purpose is to keep men ignorant of God's salvation through Christ as revealed in his Word and through the Holy Spirit. But where Christ is honored and the Holy Scriptures are professedly followed, one would expect purity of doctrine, holiness of life, and clarity of action and purpose. Instead, one finds shocking evidence of doctrines of demons (1 Timothy 4:1, 2), the result of wholesale latter-day demonic deception (1 John 4:1-6), producing dire confusion and division.[39]

To remedy this pathetic situation, the worldwide ecumenical movement, unmoored to the rock of sound doctrine, is attempting a man-made unity at the expense of revealed truth.[40] Such a venture is an open invitation to increased demonic delusion (2 Thessalonians 2:1-10), foretold by Scripture as ending in the harlot system of the false church (Revelation 17:1-18). Meanwhile, unbelief and apostasy from the faith, on one hand, open the door to lawlessness, and doctrinal credulity, on the other, augments the tragedy of an ever-growing babel of cults. Evidence mounts that only a heaven-sent spiritual revival centering in revitalized study of God's Word can alter this fatal trend.

The peril of cultism

False doctrine divides the Body of Christ. The Bible views the divisions produced by false doctrines as the chief harm caused by error introduced into the Church. Certainly it is a lamentable spectacle to see even one born-again believer separated in fellowship from another because of error and unbalanced teachings. The folly and shame of such a sight appear all the more deplorable in the light of the Bible teaching on the *oneness of all truly saved people.*

Our Lord prayed for such unity (John 17:11, 21, 22),

which was realized when the Spirit came at Pentecost (Acts 1:5; 11:14-16) to unite all God's people positionally into "one Body," the Church, by the baptism of the Spirit (1 Corinthians 12:12, 13; Romans 6:3, 4; Galatians 3:27).[41] God's people are admonished to realize experientially the unity they possess positionally before God by virtue of the Spirit's work in placing them "in Christ" (Ephesians 4:1-6; Philippians 2:2, 3). It is not surprising, therefore, that satanic powers are stubbornly directed against God's people knowing about this unity and reckoning on it so as to realize it in everyday experience. This would eliminate the harmful splits and dissensions (Galatians 5:20; 1 Corinthians 11:19; 2 Peter 2:1) that bring so much scandal upon Christian people, who are called to love one another (John 13:34) and by this love present Christ to an unbelieving world (John 13:35).

False doctrine obscures the gospel. Demonic powers do their best through human agencies to deny or distort the glorious good news of Christ's redemption. They are cunning enough to know that if they can keep men from accepting and clinging to the message of saving grace, they can completely blind their dupes. Satan knows full well that religion is a counterfeit of salvation. Accordingly, demonic powers work in religion to keep men away from salvation. Every cult and unsound sect of pseudo-Christianity is to be classified as such because it either denies or adulterates the pure gospel of grace. This is the acid test of orthodoxy (1 Corinthians 15:2, 3; Galatians 1:6-9) because it discerns the presence of demon deception diminishing the Person and finished work of Jesus Christ (1 John 4:1, 2).

Christians should stay clear of anything that diminishes the gospel of Christ and the perfect salvation it brings to those who trust Christ alone for deliverance from sin. A clear understanding of who Christ is and what he has accomplished on the cross for us will give the quiet assurance that Satan is powerless as long as we trust wholly in the Savior who has triumphed over him.

The pivotal question then is, What is the gospel? The apostle declares it is clearly revealed in the Word of God: "How that

Christ died for our sins according to the Scriptures, and that he was buried, and that he rose again the third day according to the Scriptures" (1 Corinthians 15:3, 4). "Who his own self bore our sins in his own body on the tree" (1 Peter 2:24), removing the penalty for our breaking of God's law, and justifying us totally on the basis of divine grace through faith (Romans 5:1; 8:1). So that the gospel is: "Believe on the Lord Jesus Christ (plus no other condition!) and thou shalt be saved" (Acts 16:31).

Demonic perversions are introduced the moment any other conditions whatsoever are introduced. Christ's death is absolutely and totally sufficient to save for time and eternity. Salvation includes regeneration (John 3:3, 5), baptism by the Spirit into Christ the Head (Romans 6:2, 3; 1 Corinthians 12: 12) and into his body the Church (1 Corinthians 12:13), so that the believer the moment he is saved is taken out of his position "in Adam" and placed eternally and irrevocably "in Christ" (Romans 5:11—6:11). In this position before God, the believer is dead to the condemnation of sin and alive to God "in union with Christ" (Romans 6:11). To imagine God can ever place one who is "in Christ" again "in Adam" is to allow demonic delusion to blind one to the absolutely glorious all-sufficiency of Christ's death.

Salvation, in addition to regeneration and baptism by the Spirit into mystical union with Christ and Christ's own, also includes the Spirit's sealing every believer for eternity (Ephesians 4:30) and his permanent indwelling of every believer's body as the seal (1 Corinthians 6:19, 20), with the privilege of every believer's being continually refilled with the Spirit, not merely as a second experience of the deeper life, but a constant filling following one upon another. To stop at the second experience is to fall into a satanic snare.

Salvation thus includes positional sanctification for every believer (1 Corinthians 1:1, 2), experiential sanctification being not one experience but a continual series of experiences that recognize the believer's death to sin and alive-to-God position "in Christ" (Romans 6:11), offering him moment-by-moment victory over sin through active faith (not through works).

Future sanctification (glorification) is assured every believer by virtue of what Christ alone has done for the believer, not by anything the believer can do for Christ. These are the minimal criteria defining biblical salvation.

False doctrine hinders maturity. If demonic powers are unsuccessful in keeping men away from the gospel and belief in its message, they will do all they can to disturb the believer by keeping him from looking to Jesus who is the author and finisher of our faith. In this subtle way the powers of darkness may try to hinder God's people from pressing on (being borne on by God's Spirit) to Christian "perfection," meaning "maturity" (Hebrews 6:1-3).

The Hebrew Christians — who were genuinely regenerated (Hebrews 6:4, 5) — were tempted to depart from the all-sufficiency of Christ's atonement and to return to Mosaic legalism (Hebrews 6:6). Having been saved by faith, they were nevertheless tempted to believe they must be "kept saved" at least partly by works, an error that merited severe chastening (Hebrews 6:7, 8). Like the Galatian believers, they were leaving the true gospel for "another gospel," which was in reality no gospel at all, but a satanic perversion that was keeping them from going on to maturity in Christ.

Demonism explains cultism

Demonism is the key to the plague of cultism. Christ-dishonoring cults that parade under the banner of Christianity issue from the activities of seducing spirits, producing doctrines of demons (1 Timothy 4:1, 2) and so deceiving and dividing God's people (1 John.4:1-6). False teachers and prophets are not even primarily to blame. Behind the human agent, who is visible, is the demon agent who is invisible. It is the invisible demon spirit who encourages the errors that produce disunity. Christians too often forget this fact and get their eyes off the real enemy. The results are seen in the animosities and ill-will that prevail among many Christians because they are shackled by doctrinal errors that set them off in some small sect and remove them from the pure stream of the historical biblical faith (Jude 1:3).

Sound biblicism is the cure for cultism. A biblicist is one who is versed in the Bible and who adheres to the letter and spirit of the Bible. Sound biblicism honors the Bible as the fully inspired and authoritative Word of God (2 Timothy 3:16, 17) and relies upon the author, the Holy Spirit, to teach its revealed truth (John 16:12, 13); yet the biblicist fully equips himself linguistically, historically, theologically, and logically to be a competent expositor. The sound biblicist dares to accept the Bible on its own claims as he would any other piece of logically written literature, assuming that it has plan and purpose and time periods within which certain truths and events must be placed to understand them in their context and setting.

Failure in this manner to deal fairly and rationally with the Bible text is a prolific source of error that has spawned many unsound doctrines that burgeoned into sects based on ignorance and refusal to honor God's Word in a common sense way.[42] The Word can be honored only by inductive logic — allowing the Bible to speak explicitly in the details and then to form the general, far-ranging truths from the details. Deductive logic that first formulates a teaching and then forces the Bible details to support it or ignores details that cannot be fitted into the teaching is a prominent spawning ground of cultism. Also prolific in producing errors and divisions among Christians is the practice of substituting "church tradition" and ecclesiastical "decisions" for plain pronouncements of the Word of God.

Demon powers lie in wait to produce and promulgate "doctrines of demons" and divisions among the saints the moment sound biblicism is compromised. Demons can bypass men's opinions, church traditions, ecclesiastical decisions, and anything and everything except the Word of God itself as it reveals Jesus Christ. Had the Christ of the Scriptures been fully honored, none of the motley babel of cults that plague Christianity would have come into being. It is just as certain that if the Word of God were fully honored and a sound biblicism adhered to, every error and cult now parading under the banner of Christ would vanish. God's true people would become one in practice and profession as they are one in their position before God in union with Christ (John 17:11, 20, 21; Ephesians 4:1-6).

Satan knows full well the strength there is in unity. It is high time Christians realize the same and see clearly who is responsible for their disunity, and as a result resolve to return to a sound biblicism. The choice is inexorable. Shall we take a course away from the Bible to follow a false "ecumenical" unity that will eventuate in ecclesiastical Babylon, ripened for destruction (Revelation 17:1-18) as Satan's bride? Or shall we take the road back to the Bible and the true unity of the Church, the Body and Bride of Christ? If the latter, we shall be prepared for dynamic service in a world of needy sinners while the Lord delays his coming, and we will be ready to meet him and be glorified when he comes to receive us to himself (1 Thessalonians 4:13-18; 1 John 3:1-3).

NOTES
CHAPTER 8

1. E. B. Tylor, *Primitive Culture*, 1: 424.
2. J. G. Frazer, *The Golden Bough*, 3rd ed. (1911-1915), 1: 222.
3. Robert R. Marett, "Religion," *Encyclopaedia Britannica*, 19 (1964): 103.
4. George Galloway, "Religion," *Encyclopaedia Britannica*, 19 (1964): 110.
5. *Ibid.*
6. Cf. R. H. Codrington, *The Melanesians;* W. B. Spencer and F. J. Gillen, *The Native Tribes of Central Australia*, and *The Northern Tribes of Central Australia;* A. B. Ellis, *The Tshi-Speaking People of the Gold Coast;* E. Westermarck, *Ritual and Belief in Morocco;* R. H. Lowie, *Primitive Religion.*
7. For primitive religious ideas in a highly developed pagan culture see J. J. M. DeGroot, *The Religious System of China;* John Nevius, *Demon Possession.*
8. Galloway, p. 107, column 1.
9. Galloway, p. 107, column 2.
10. Cf. the Hebrew expression, *lo' 'elohim,* "no-gods" (Jeremiah 2:11; 5:7; 16:20).
11. Edward Langton, *Essentials of Demonology*, p. 185; cf. also pp. 183-186; Merrill F. Unger, *Biblical Demonology*, 9th ed., p. 170.
12. A. R. Fausset, *Jamieson, Fausset, Brown Commentary*, 4: 312.

13. *Ibid.*

14. An example is Asclepius, the Greek god of medicine and healing, mentioned by Homer in the *Iliad* only as a skilled physician, but afterward honored as a hero and eventually worshiped as a god; Alice Walton, "The Cult of Asklepios," *Cornell Studies of Classical Philology* 3 (1894). Another example is Hercules (Greek, Herakles), the most famous Greek legendary hero, later deified (cf. K. Latte, *Römische Religionsgeschichte* (1960), pp. 213 ff.).

15. Published by William Benton, *Encyclopaedia Britannica*, p. 710.

16. Jan K. Van Baalen, *The Chaos of the Cults*, 7th ed., p. 297.

17. For a study of the ecumenical trend see W. A. Visser t'Hooft, *The Meaning of Ecumenical;* R. Rouse and S. C. Neill, eds., *A History of the Ecumenical Movement 1517-1948;* S. C. Neill, *Towards Church Union, 1937-1952; The Ecumenical Review*, 1948-1970.

18. See *The Church, The Churches, and The World Council of Churches*, by the Central Committee of the World Council of Churches (1950); N. Goodall, *The Ecumenical Movement* (1961).

19. Stuart P. Garver, "The Challenge of the Seventies," *Christian Heritage*, 31, no. 1 (January 1970): 5.

20. Garver, *loc. cit.*

21. William Hoste, Appendix 2, "What Should Be the Attitude of Christian Missionaries Towards Other Religions?" in *Heresies Exposed*, William Irvine, comp., 11th ed. (1940), p. 219.

22. For a study of the subject see W. T. deBary, ed., *Sources of Indian Tradition;* L. S. O'Malley, *Popular Hinduism.*

23. Arthur L. Basham, "Hinduism," *Encyclopaedia Britannica*, 11 (1965): 507, 508. Cf. Malcolm Pitt, *Introducing Hinduism.*

24. As a result of growing apostasy from the Christian faith, many Americans are being lured by a wide spectrum of new religions; see "The Search for Faith," *Life*, 68, no. 1 (January 9, 1970): 16-26.

25. *Ibid.*, pp. 17, 24, 25.

26. *Ibid.*, p. 25. But we ask, "Is religion to 'get one high' or to get one saved? Is it 'do-it-yourself' (salvation by works, the false gospel) or 'let-God-do-it' (salvation by faith, the true gospel)?" This attitude differentiates true religion from the false, the demonic from the divine.

27. Wing-tsit Chan, "Confucianism," *Encyclopaedia Britannica*, 6 (1964): 308.

28. E. J. Thomas, *The Road to Nirvana*, selected scriptures from the Pali; W. Woodville Rockhill, trans., *The Life of the Buddha and the Early History of His Order*, derived from Tibetan works; Thomas, trans., *The Quest of Enlightenment*, selected scriptures from the Sanskrit.

29. Cf. Lin Yutang, ed. and trans., *The Wisdom of Lao-tse.*

30. W. E. Sothill, *Three Religions of China;* cf. also R. K. Douglas, *Confucianism and Taoism.*

31. Clarence H. Hamilton, "Buddhism," *Encyclopaedia Britannica*, (1964): 357.

32. See W. G. Aston, *Shinto — The Way of the Gods;* D. C. Holtom, *The National Faith of Japan,* and *Modern Japan and Shinto Nationalism,* rev. ed., 1947.

33. See H. Lammens, *Islam: Beliefs and Institutions,* trans., E. Dension Ross; A. Wensinck, Jr., *The Muslim Creed;* H. A. R. Gibb, *Mohammedanism;* A. S. Tritton, *Muslim Theology.* See also Gibb, *Modern Trends in Islam.*

34. Cf. C. C. Torrey, *The Jewish Foundation of Islam.*

35. Cf. Isidore Epstein, "Judaism," *Encyclopaedia Britannica,* (1964): 165-168.

36. Epstein, *loc. cit.*

37. Epstein, *loc. cit.*

38. For a study of demonic delusion and Jewish unbelief, see Merrill F. Unger, *Biblical Demonology,* 9th ed., pp. 210-213.

39. Cf. Jan K. Van Baalen, *Chaos of Cults;* Elmer T. Clark, *The Small Sects of America,* rev. ed., 1949.

40. Cf. S. C. Neill, *Towards Church Union 1937-1952; The Ten Formative Years,* published by the World Council of Churches; N. Goodall, *The Ecumenical Movement;* M. Villain, *Introduction à l'occumenisme.*

41. For a study of the baptism of the Holy Spirit and its connection with salvation and Christian unity, see Merrill F. Unger, *The Baptizing Work of the Holy Spirit,* pp. 1-136.

42. For a discussion of sound principles of Bible interpretation, see the author's *Principles of Expository Preaching,* pp. 11-252.

Demons and Deliverance

Scripture clearly reveals that as a result of Adam's fall into sin, the human race has been exposed to the power of Satan and demons. Demonic power over fallen man, however, is severely restricted within limits the Creator has ordained. But when men violate the moral laws of God, they subject themselves to the satanic yoke that binds them in opposition to God and brings them under the sway of occult powers in the hidden realm of evil supernaturalism. This sphere of the occult invades the natural realm of physical laws through human beings who have exposed themselves to satanic power.

Occult enslavement varies in severity and intensity, depending upon the extent to which the moral law of God has been violated and the Creator dishonored by complicity with occult arts such as spiritism, fortune-telling, and magic, or by involvement in demonic cults where diabolic power deludes and enslaves. Sometimes occult enslavement may not be traceable to the conduct or actions of the afflicted one at all, but may be the result of occult complicity on the part of his forebears, with the occult taint unexpectedly cropping out, like some physical maladies that run in families.

During the present worldwide revival of occultism, occult subjection is becoming a very common phenomenon. Practices which were once conducted in secret and abhorred by the average person, as sorcery, are now presented under the cloak of respectability and popularized in the theater, the movies, on television and radio, and in literature. As a result, multitudes are upset emotionally, mentally, and physically. Although treatment by psychiatry or psychology may help many, the occult factor tends more and more to take the matter beyond the province of the secular psychologist and psychiatrist and to place it in the hands of the Christian pastor and counselor. The latter, as a teacher of the Christian gospel of liberation, has the necessary concern and knowledge to deal with the problems of occult enslavement and can point to Christ as the way of deliverance.

Prevalence of occult subjection

There is a reason why occultism and the "black arts" are enjoying a wide revival. Occult studies and practices have always been cultivated in certain areas of the world. But today the occult revival invades traditional Christian society, where a departure from a Christ-centered Christianity produces spiritual vacuity. People look for meaning and fulfillment in such things as witchcraft, magic, and sorcery that finds expression in Tarot card reading, playing with the Ouija board, spiritistic séances, levitation of bodies, table lifting, and innumerable other psychic practices and experiments.[1]

England is witnessing a revival of the occult that threatens to engulf it in the spiritual darkness of the Middle Ages. Thousands of self-admitted "witches" (spiritistic mediums) meet regularly to perpetrate pagan rituals, fertility rites, and to invoke and worship pagan gods, who are demons (Deuteronomy 32:16, 17; 1 Corinthians 10:20).

In the January 9, 1970, issue of *Life* appears a picture of "Elizabeth," one of 500 "witches" living in Manhattan. "She is a 'white witch,' a 'good witch,' as opposed to black witches, who are evil."[2] Elizabeth prefers to remain anonymous "because there is so much interest in witchcraft these days she fears her life would not be her own if her identity were known."[3] She has been practicing serious witchcraft for fifteen years. Her mother, who was a witch, passed the art on to her. She attends weekly coven meetings, reads Tarot cards, prepares love potions for friends, and casts "beneficial spells." To her, "witchcraft is a religion like any other." She uses oils, incense, and herbs for conjurations and always has ready her black book of incantations.

Occult subjection among the unregenerate

The vulnerability of the unsaved. Although born-again believers who dabble in the occult are not immune from its perils, unbelievers are particularly vulnerable. This does not mean that unsaved humanity is completely at the mercy of Satan and demons. There is a rigid divine curb on the powers of darkness even in the case of men who do not know Christ's redemptive power. Satan and demonic forces can deceive men and keep them from God's saving grace in Christ, but as long as they avoid God-dishonoring idolatry and occultism (Exodus 20:3-5; Deuteronomy 18:10-12), they are not subject to the occult deception and enslavement that inevitably results from idolatrous apostasy.

Because present-day apostasy represents an idolatrous departure from God's Word, it is being accompanied by widespread occult interest and practice presenting a peril of unparalleled proportions to the unwary. For if men consider the eternal moral law of God no longer binding, but Victorian and passé, the so-called "new morality" will turn out to be nothing more than the old immorality of debauched and occult-ridden paganism.

If men believe that God is "dead" and that they do not owe their Creator supreme love and loyalty,[4] there is no deterrent to keep them from dabbling in the occult, which is the natural expression of a lawless spirit. Setting aside love for God, such men soon abandon any concern for their fellowman. Failure to keep the first table of commandments inevitably leads to failure to keep the second one. Spiritual lawlessness, in which occultism and false religionism flourish, goes hand in hand with moral lawlessness. Crime skyrockets and social evils abound in such a troubled era. Occult revival starts and prospers in a morally and spiritually sick society.

Increase of occult subjection and the witness of Scripture.

The Scriptures predict a tremendous upsurge of demonism in the closing days of the Church age that will produce the great apostasy and the rise of innumerable demon-inspired cults (1 Timothy 4:1-6; 1 John 4:1-7), as well as general lawlessness and rampant immorality throughout Christendom (cf. 2 Timothy 3:1-9). The apostle connects this moral sag with occult revival and consequent psychic oppression by referring to Jannes and Jambres, the Egyptian magicians and demon workers. "Just as Jannes and Jambres opposed Moses," declares Paul, apostate religious teachers of the end time "oppose the truth, corrupt thinkers as they are and counterfeits so far as faith is concerned" (2 Timothy 3:8, Berkeley).

The apostle plainly indicates that the Spirit of God resident in the true Church, the Body of Christ, would hold back the full manifestation of the end-time outburst of demon power until he would leave the world to present the completed Church to Christ (2 Thessalonians 2:7) at the end of the age.[5] Then with the Church glorified and removed to heaven, and the Holy Spirit's restraining power largely removed from earth, the "mystery of iniquity" will be revealed, precipitating an outburst of evil supernaturalism from the Antichrist, the lawless one.

"The coming of the lawless one is according to Satan's working, with great powers and signs and miracles, all of them false, and with limitless deceit of wickedness for those who, because they did not welcome the love of the truth for their salvation, are going to destruction. And for this reason God visits them with a delusion that operates on them to believe the falsehood, so that all who have not believed the truth but have taken pleasure in wickedness may receive judgment" (2 Thessalonians 2:9-11, Berkeley).

"The falsehood" (lie) these unbelieving religionists are deluded into believing is the personal Antichrist (John 5:43). This is the penalty for rejecting "the love of the truth" which was available while the Church was still upon the earth. Subscribing to the occult religions that flourish in the midst of the great apostasy from the "faith once for all delivered to the saints" (Jude 3), they will reject the true Christ and the gospel of salvation by grace through faith in his finished work on the cross. This will expose them to the deluding doctrines of demons that will not only keep them away from God's salvation but seal them in the ruin that overtakes the devil's dupes at the end time.

The second advent of Christ to take over the rule of the earth (Revelation 19:11-16) will be preceded by a desperate, colossal attempt of Satan to delude and dominate unregenerate humanity and take over the rule of this globe. The evil one will be assisted in this nefarious scheme by myriads of vile spirits let loose from the abyss during the Great Tribulation (Revelation 9:1-21) who will delude, torment, and drive men to devil worship and all kinds of occultism. As Satan and his hosts are expelled from the heavenlies to the earth (Revelation 12:7-9), they will vent great wrath, knowing that their time is short. Working through the Antichrist (Revelation 13:1-10) and the False Prophet (Revelation 13:11-18), they will exhibit a full array of deceptive miracles to incite men to battle at Armageddon (Revelation 16:13, 14), representing the supremely foolhardy goal of banishing the name of God and of Christ from the earth and taking over the globe in Satan's name.

The personal advent of Christ will crush this monstrous, demon-inspired uprising. Satan and his diabolical hordes will be thrown into the abyss (Zechariah 13:2; Revelation 20:1-3), resulting in the final destruction of the satanic world system in which Satan and his minions have operated since the fall. The kingdom of God and his Christ will then take the place of the satanic world system.[6]

Results of increasing occult subjection in the end time. The degree to which unregenerate humanity is exposed to psychic enslavement in the latter-day occult revival is fearful. Vulnerable and unprotected by faith in Christ's redemptive victory, unsaved people become a ready pawn of the devil, particularly as they take up with some phase of the occult arts or some aspect of occult religion.

The Apostle Paul foresaw the general moral decline that would accompany this increased activity of the powers of darkness and solemnly warned God's people of the impending peril. "Know this, though, that in the last days there are troublous times impending. For people will be self-lovers, avaricious, boasters, haughty, abusive, disobedient to parents, ungrateful, irreverent, without natural affection, relentless, slanderers, uncontrolled, brutal, with no love for the good, treacherous, rash, conceited, pleasure-loving rather than God-loving. While retaining a form of piety, they are strangers to its power" (2 Timothy 3:1-5, Berkeley).

Retaining the outward form or shell of orthodox godliness, people will deny Christ's inner power and spiritual reality. Without the guidance of the Holy Spirit and the redemptive power of Christ, dupes of Satan will be blinded and confirmed in false teaching by demonic duplicity and power.

What this will mean is viewed by the apocalyptic seer. "And the rest of the men who were not killed by these plagues yet repented not of the works of their hands, that they should not worship demons, and idols of gold, and silver, and bronze and wood, which neither can see, nor hear, nor walk. Neither repented they of their murders, nor of their sorceries, nor of their fornication, nor of their thefts" (Revelation 9:20, 21).

This passage describes the character and fruitage of the occult religionism that will dominate the false, harlot church after the true, virgin Church has been taken to heaven. Such occult religion will center in demon-energized idolatry and will be cultivated by the ungodly, who, like Pharaoh hardening his heart against the judgments of the Lord, will remain completely unrepentant in the face of the awful apocalyptic visitations of the Great Tribulation. Despite the excruciating torments caused by the "demon-locusts" under the fifth trumpet (Revelation 9:1-12), and the decimation of one-third of the earth's population by the infernal cavalry under the sixth trumpet (Revelation 9:13-19), the hardened sinners who remain will not repent of their God-dishonoring worship of "the works of their own hands" (Deuteronomy 31:29), especially the idols made by their hands (cf. Revelation 13:14, 15; 19:20).

Such idolatry is demon worship, because behind the visible idol is the invisible god (demon), energizing its worship (1

Corinthians 10:20). The fruits of such demon worship are listed as (1) "murders," that is, violence and crime of every sort (2) "sorceries," specifically witchcraft by means of drugs (Galatians 5:20). "In sorcery, the use of drugs, whether simple or potent, was generally accompanied by incantations and appeals to occult powers, with the provision of various charms, amulets, etc., professedly designed to keep the suppliant or patient from the attention of the power of demons, but actually to impress the suppliant with the mysterious resources and powers of the sorcerer."[7]

(3) "Fornication" (singular). The other sins (plural) are perpetuated at intervals and show the moral results of the operation of occult powers through demon-energized religion. Those ensnared in moral impurity and sexual lawlessness indulge in perpetual fornication, which is characteristic of occult religionism (cf. 2 Timothy 3:6-9). (4) "Thefts" show that where the moral law of God is abandoned, Satan the liar, murderer, and thief reproduces his character in those who worship him (cf. John 8:44).

Occult subjection among the regenerate

Why occult subjection is prevalent among Christians. Christians can and ought to enjoy complete deliverance from the power of Satan and demons as a result of Christ's perfect work of redemption. But what believers can and ought to enjoy and what they actually do enjoy are two different things. When Christians fail to recognize what they have in Christ and refuse to appropriate the resulting privileges, they invite defeat and can be held captive by demonic forces to a pitiable degree.

Occult subjection among Christians is prevalent for several reasons. The Christian need not fear Satan because he believes in Christ's redemptive work. This is precisely why Satan attacks him. The believer need only remember that he is strong in Christ (Ephesians 1:3; 6:10-20), and need not be defeated or even oppressed by principalities, powers, rulers of this age's darkness, and wicked spirits (demons) in the heavenly realms (Ephesians 6:12). The Christian adage is, "Stand against Satan or be invaded by Satan." Just as our Lord was the target for Satan's attack while here on earth (Matthew 4:1-11) so the believer, now joined to his Lord vitally and spiritually, becomes the target for satanic onslaught.

The center of the believer's sphere of operation, "in the heavenly places in Christ" (Ephesians 1:3) becomes a victorious battleground when the privileges and benefits of that sphere are understood from the Word and claimed by faith. The alternative that faces the believer is inexorable. If he does not stand against Satan in victorious conflict, he will be afflicted and oppressed by Satan in ignominious defeat. In the present day of apostasy and revival of the occult arts under the guise of religion, few Christians are conducting a victorious warfare. Many are succumbing to the enemy through sin, carnal appetites, and complicity with some aspect of occult-oriented religionism. The result is that psychic oppression is not only rampant among the unsaved but widespread among not merely professing Christians but born-again believers.[8]

The manifestation of occult oppression among Christians. The fact that believers can be oppressed by demon powers and actually suffer infestation by evil spirits is not only attested by the Scriptures but by contemporary human experience. Job was severely afflicted physically as well as materially (Job 1: 1—2:10). King Saul was a Spirit-anointed leader of the Lord's people, yet became indwelt by an evil spirit that hounded him to insane jealousy, hatred, and murder, and finally drove him to resort to witchcraft, which he himself had outlawed from his realm in obedience to the law of Moses (Leviticus 19:30; 20:6; 1 Samuel 28:3; 1 Chronicles 10:13). Believers are in peril of being trapped by "the snare of the devil" and being "taken captive by him at his will" (cf. 2 Timothy 2:23-26). A believer, "a daughter of Abraham," had been bound by a "spirit of infirmity" eighteen years when set free by Jesus (Luke 13:11-13). The incestuous believer at Corinth was undoubtedly possessed with an unclean spirit, being guilty of a sexual offence not even mentioned among godless pagans (1 Corinthians 5:1-5).

Everyday experience adds its testimony to that of the Scripture that believers can be oppressed and enslaved by demon powers. Kurt E. Koch in counseling thousands of occultly oppressed people found innumerable cases of Christians needing deliverance from occult subjection.[9] Hobart E. Freeman, a pastor, declares, "In my personal experience, the majority of those for whom I have prayed for deliverance from occult oppression or subjection were Christians, including ministers and the wives of ministers."[10]

Believers can be hindered, bound, and oppressed by Satan and even indwelt by one or more demons, who may derange the mind and afflict the body. This does not mean, of course, that all physical or mental ills are caused by demon spirits. But it does mean that certain ones may be caused by demons, and when the demon is expelled the particular mental or physical malady is removed. Scripture presents demons as possessing power over the human body to cause dumbness (Matthew 12:22), insanity (Luke 8:26-36), suicidal mania (Mark 9:22), and various physical defects and deformities (Luke 13:11-17).

The writer during many years of pastoral ministry and counseling has witnessed the grip Satan can hold over truly regenerated believers. He has often noted that some believers are delivered from evil spirits when they are saved, others are not, and must be delivered later by fasting and prayer. Others struggle on in the Christian life, never completely set free from demon power.[11] One prominent woman in the church, a tireless and consecrated worker for Christ, was nevertheless possessed by a spirit of intense jealousy and spite, from which so far as the writer knows she was never delivered. She finally ended up in a church unsound in doctrine and practice.

Another woman, who excelled in the gift of intercessory prayer, was nevertheless constantly the center of a disturbance because of lack of tact and wisdom, due apparently to some alien spirit indwelling her. The writer remembers well the occasion of a prayer meeting when this woman was delivered from this evil spirit, as she and a group were upon their knees in intercession. All of a sudden, as she quietly prayed, the demon in her gave an unearthly yell that could be heard for a block and came out of her, frightening the group almost out of their wits. After falling into an unconscious state for a minute or two, the woman regained consciousness and rose to her feet, joyfully confident that she had been set free from an evil power. Such an instance recalls Luke's account of "certain women who had been healed of evil spirits and infirmities," of whom the first recorded is Mary Magdelene, from whom "seven demons had gone out" (Luke 8:2).

Another interesting case comes to mind concerning a professing Christian father of a large family, among the members of which the Lord was signally working in salvation and blessings. Although the father had made a profession of Christ, and no doubt was genuinely saved, he was nevertheless very immature in faith and afflicted with a violent temper which he seemed unable to control. On one occasion I had opportunity to observe him, unnoticed by him, in one of these violent paroxysms and was amazed to hear another voice speaking and cursing within the man, indication enough that his violent passion was the result of demon inhabitation.

Probably the most astonishing cases of occult enslavement of Christians concern those who are trapped in false doctrine, especially in error concerning deeper spiritual living and who parade as apostles of light. One such example comes from my first pastorate. This woman, truly born again but ill-instructed in the nature and content of Christ's salvation, taught a second experience of power that was evidenced, she claimed, by speaking in supernatural languages. The pride and divisiveness of this woman bore the most evident stamp of demonic deception and enslavement. Her type of subtle, demonic delusion is very dangerous, for it hides under a halo instead of a diabolical horn.

That many regenerated people need to claim deliverance from evil spirits indwelling them is a fact that we would prefer to think is not true, but which is all too true and must be faced realistically by pastors and counselors who would lay claim to competence and effectiveness in discharging their high and holy calling. In a time when occult religionism is enjoying a tremendous revival, some Christians are bound to become occultly involved and contaminated. If Christian pastors fail to help the occultly oppressed, who will be able to help?

Deliverance from occult subjection

Deliverance from occult enslavement challenges both the local church and its occultly afflicted member. Each has his own function to perform, if Christian people are to enjoy the freedom from satanic powers that the gospel of grace guarantees the believer. The sad truth is that, due to liberal theology, the reality of Satan and demons is widely denied today, so that many professing Christians cannot cope with their enemy because they refuse to recognize he exists. Such denials, of course, do not affect the existence of the powers of darkness. They exist no matter how sincerely their nonexistence is insisted upon. Avowals of their nonexistence serve to accentuate the ignorance of so many in a realm where to be ignorant is to be imperiled (cf. 2 Corinthians 2:11).

Responsibility of the Church

The Church should expose the craft and power of demonic spirits and point to the way of deliverance. This is a far cry from the foolish delusion of the false prophets who insist, "There is no personal Devil, nor demons!" How can a professing church warn against the enemy or expose his craft when it denies the existence of that enemy? This is the tragic situation in a segment of the church where liberalizing theology has no gospel of deliverance nor any knowledge of Satan and demon powers. Such a false church is at the mercy of demonic powers and can offer no deliverance to members when they are in the satanic web of occult religion.

Even in evangelical circles, where Satan and demons are recognized as existing, an atmosphere of make-believe prevails with regard to the extensive influence these malevolent spirits exercise against the human race. Though tacitly, the unscriptural idea is widely entertained that demonism presents no serious threat to the Christian today. The general truth that Christ defeated Satan and demon powers at Calvary is popularly presented (Colossians 1:13), but the believer's need for constant reliance upon God and use of spiritual armor is left unexplained. Consequently, the intensity of spiritual conflict and the disastrous results of defeat are little recognized, and many believers fall victim to Satan because they are not aware of his presence!

Many evangelicals have a very imperfect concept of the power and operation of Satan. As far as his demon helpers are concerned, Christians vaguely recognize the existence of evil spirits, but have no clear notion of their role in human conduct and the responsibility of the Church as endowed with the necessary powers and authority from the risen Christ and through the outpoured gift of the Spirit to conduct an effective warfare against these powers of darkness. Casting out demons, binding the forces of evil, and loosing victims from satanic enslavement are continuing needs, not activities relegated to the ministry of Christ and the early Church.

Every Spirit-anointed minister should echo the words of the Great Deliverer, the Lord Jesus Christ, whose wonderful ministry of liberation was so gloriously foretold by the prophet Isaiah. "The Spirit of the Lord God is upon me, for the Lord has anointed me to preach good tidings to the afflicted. He has sent me to heal the brokenhearted; to proclaim liberty to the captives and opening of the prison to those who are bound, to proclaim the year of the Lord's favor" (Isaiah 61: 1, 2; Hebrew; cf. Luke 4:18, 19).

The Church is responsible to use its charismatic gifts of healing and deliverance. The scriptural teaching on the gifts of the Spirit (1 Corinthians 12—14) has fared very badly in the present-day Church, the result of two extreme views, one involving deliberate unbelief, the other ignorant credulity. As a result of the first view, the Church has been encouraged to abandon its belief in the need of charismatic gifts today, reasoning that they were merely a kind of temporary foundation for the erection of the first-century Church.

While the temporary nature of three of the nine gifts catalogued in 1 Corinthians 12:7-11, namely, direct inspirational prophecy, supernatural languages, and direct inspirational wisdom, is definitely indicated in the passage itself (1 Corinthians 13:8), nothing is said of the temporary nature of the other gifts, notably, "gifts of healings" (Greek) (1 Corinthians 12: 9). These were to continue throughout the Church age, even after "the completed (final) thing" — the inspired New Testament Scriptures — would be given (1 Corinthians 13:10) rendering unnecessary direct inspirational prophecies and knowledge and messages in other languages.

Ignorant credulity, on the other hand, steadfastly refuses to face the clear teaching of the passage on the temporary nature of three of these gifts and to recognize the obvious fact that, when the completed New Testament Scriptures became available, these gifts were superseded and no longer needed. That which formerly had been given by the Spirit in direct inspirational prophecies and knowledge and through supernatural languages would now be recorded for posterity in the written Scriptures. The gifts now needed would be discernment of the sacred oracles themselves and expository gifts of preaching and teaching the written Word (cf. Ephesians 4:11, 12).

When we remind the Church of its obligation to use its charismatic gifts of healing to deliver those chained by satanic powers, we need to point out that this gift is not included in the temporary list. It was meant to continue throughout the Church age because it would be needed throughout this entire period, even after the New Testament Scripture would be written and circulated among the churches.

It should be carefully noted that casting out of demons is not a spiritual gift nor the peculiar ability of a few Spirit-filled believers. It is the prerogative of all who trust and sincerely follow Christ, but it is obviously closely connected with the Church's charismatic power to heal ("gifts of healings," 1

Corinthians 12:9, Greek) and with the effective outreach of the gospel (Mark 16:15-20). Inhabitation by evil spirits is always accompanied by physical, mental, or emotional instability, and the casting out of demons is always a species of healing, although clearly to be distinguished from healing of body and mind, apart from demon inhabitation (cf. Matthew 8:16, 17).

The Church was called and endowed with the requisite power and authority to conduct an effective warfare against the powers of darkness (Matthew 16:18). The risen Christ in conquest over the spirit world (Colossians 1:13) commissioned his disciples with the glowing words: "All power is given unto me in heaven and in earth. Go ye, therefore, and teach all nations" (Matthew 28:18, 19). Certainly there is no excuse for the Church to surrender its charismatic power to heal and deliver from satanic oppression. In the very measure that it does, it advertises its spiritual bankruptcy and makes itself a weak institution that no longer commands the respect of the spiritually needy masses. No wonder multitudes are seeking spiritual reality in Oriental religions, non-Christian faiths and occult-oriented perversions of Christianity.[12] Christian faith is so devitalized by apostasy and so contaminated with men's opinions and a defective presentation of Jesus Christ that it is becoming a hollow shell, powerless to affect men's lives.

The Church is responsible to furnish spiritually and intellectually competent leadership in the ministry of salvation and deliverance from the powers of evil. As a result of forfeiting a clear presentation of Christ's redemptive power and of not using its charismatic power to heal and to deliver from satanic oppression today, the pastoral ministry becomes no more effective than the secular role of the clinical psychologist, the social worker, or the humanistic philosopher. The tragic result is that people who suffer from spiritual, mental, physical, or psychic disorders, which only Christ can really cure, are turned over to other professionals for medical or psychotherapeutic treatment which cannot reach the heart of the matter.

Jack C. Oakes III, pastor of the College Hill Presbyterian Church, Oxford, Mississippi, aptly remarks: "The church in secular form is no church at all. This becomes most apparent

when campus ministers devoid of a faith capable of transcend-
ing the boundaries of humanism, are forced to 'seek meaning
and fulfillment' in secular roles. Most of them are unprepared
to act as clinical psychologists, social workers, and philoso-
phers. Those who do have the necessary credentials are often
better off when they drop their religious trappings."[13]

When the Church began to lose sight of the exceeding sinfulness of sin and the glory of Christ's redemption, it steadily
began to lose ground to the powers of darkness in country after country. The more sin has been minimized and Satan
mythologized, the more insidious have been the inroads these
evil powers have been making into the professing Church. Only
as God's people arouse themselves to pray and return to the
gospel of redemptive grace as revealed in Jesus Christ will the
Church be able to stem and overcome the present-day flood of
demonic wickedness sweeping across the earth.

An effective ministry of deliverance, especially from occult
subjection, must include knowledge and genuine faith in
Christ. The knowledge must comprise not only knowledge of
the Word and will of God (spiritual knowledge) but technical
knowledge as well, especially the science of human psychology and the general sphere of psychiatry. This equipment
is essential to establish a correct diagnosis of psychic ailments.
Their causes could be of a purely medical nature, or result
from occult subjection, or present a combination of both factors. Prime importance must be attached to medical causes in
the psychic patient, and when they are suspected, the patient
must be referred to a medical specialist.

If, on the other hand, diagnosis discloses a combination of
medical and occult causes, then collaboration is required with
a psychologist or psychiatrist, preferably one who acknowl-
edges the spiritual and occult problems in the phenomena.
In the case of psychic disturbance without any medical aspects, a clear case of occult subjection is attested. Then the
gospel of delivering grace through Christ must be brought to
bear upon the patient and release sought in the power of
Christ through faith and prayer.

Dr. Kurt Koch relates the case of a well-known, successful

business man who came to him after an evangelistic sermon to make a spontaneous disclosure of psychic trouble. The patient would confine himself for days in a dark room, losing all interest in his work, with his whole outlook clouded with gloom. Medical findings of periodic melancholia, however, turned out to be only part of the man's problem. Dr. Koch suspected some occult relationship as well, despite the initial indication that the patient's ancestors were pious folk, faithful people of the church. Careful examination of the family and forebears disclosed a nephew with a similar melancholic condition, a grandfather who was a magic practitioner, banning sicknesses and a conjurer of cattle, who died in an insane asylum, as well as a sister and aunt who were suicides.

Such a familiar pattern of depression furnishes the psychiatrist with a typical form for the inheriting of manic-depressive insanity.[14] The pastoral counselor dealing with cases of occult involvement knows it can often be traced back to three or four generations. There it is normal to find the pattern of deaths in insane asylums, melancholia, suicide, and fatal accidents.[15]

This example of a mixed type shows that sound psychiatric treatment must be pursued along with special spiritual guidance in the gospel of Christ's deliverance. It also demonstrates the necessity of differential diagnosis. Equipped with spiritual insight as well as all scientific help, the man of God is called upon to present Jesus Christ to sin-chained and demon-enslaved humanity.

Responsibility of the occultly oppressed

The Church as a divine institution ministering for Christ (Acts 1:1) and functioning in behalf of human need as the Body of Christ (1 Corinthians 12:12-26), fulfills its duty when it offers men deliverance from sin and the powers of darkness. But it is one thing to offer deliverance to the occultly oppressed; it is quite another thing for those bound by evil powers to accept and appropriate the deliverance offered and to enter into the sphere of freedom guaranteed by Christ's redemptive work. To obtain actual emancipation from satanic control, the occultly oppressed must reach out in faith and receive the deliverance the Church offers in and through Jesus Christ.

The occultly oppressed must confess faith in Christ as Savior. This is the starting point! For Christ on the cross triumphed over evil supernaturalism, and any genuine victory must be obtained through faith in his redemptive work as we are united by faith to him, the Victor (1 Corinthians 12:12, 13; Romans 6:3, 4; Colossians 2:8-10; Galatians 3:27; Ephesians 1:3-12; 6:10-20). Sometimes the occultly enslaved seek relief with no real interest in salvation or in following Christ. They cannot be liberated. Living faith in Christ's perfect salvation is the only antidote that will vanquish satanic power.

This is why the apostle urges victorious, Spirit-filled believers to "be strong in the Lord, and in the power of his might" (Ephesians 6:10). The idea is not "be strong in strength received from the Lord" but "your strength must come from your position and place in the Lord." All regenerated believers "in Christ" are in a sphere of strength, which is the triumphant Christ himself (Colossians 1:13). Only he who conquered the powers of darkness can deliver us from satanic attacks.

The inability of the victim to confess Christ is symptomatic of occult subjection. Accordingly, in such cases, the oppressed person, under the dominion of dark powers, must be encouraged to confess Christ as Lord and Savior by those who are praying for him and standing with him for liberation. The procedure should be to have the victim repeat after them the words of such a confession. To wonder about the sincerity of such a confession is pointless. If the occultly oppressed person were not in earnest, he would not be seeking liberation in the first place.

It must be remembered that demonic powers seek to keep the occult victim from believing God and trusting Christ who they know (Romans 10:9, 10) will liberate him from their slavery (James 4:7; 1 Peter 5:9), bringing the light and power of God's salvation. Sometimes, when the patient is severely oppressed and definitely indwelt by one or more demons, prolonged prayer will be a prelude to any deliverance. The efficacy of the blood of Jesus must be pleaded, and the battle waged incessantly before the victim will be able to frame a confession of faith with his lips and have faith generated in his heart.

The Rev. J. A. MacMillan gives an account of a present-day deliverance from very severe demon oppression, or actually demon possession, since the patient suffered periods of unconsciousness (coma) in which her senses were bound, and the resident evil spirits took charge of her, actually speaking out of her body.[16] The victim in this instance was a sincere but poorly instructed believer who upon the fairly recent death of her mother had sought the services of a spiritistic medium. She naïvely believed that this was good and could help her communicate with her departed loved one. Little did she realize how directly she was breaking God's commands (Exodus 20:3-5; Leviticus 19:31; 20:6; Deuteronomy 18:10, 11) and opening herself to occult enslavement.

The medium quickly discovered that her visitor was highly psychic. Before long she asked her to unite with her in certain trance experiences, and later obtained her cooperation in her spiritistic séances, inducing her to yield to the will of the spirits. It was then that the woman found herself occultly bound and .in serious psychic trouble. She sought spiritual help from her pastor, who called together a group of Christians to pray for the deliverance of this woman.

The struggle lasted for several months, with seven nights spent in prayer. The sufferer was unable to claim the Lord's help for herself, intense fear paralyzing her mind. At intervals, when the struggle in prayer was being waged, she would come briefly out of the coma in which her senses were bound. When she was urged to confess the name of Jesus and praise God, she would try to do so but immediately the spirits would use the victim's own hands in a fierce endeavor to strangle her. Two strong Christian men were constantly alert at her side to hold her when she became violent. At other moments, she would attempt to bite those about her, as an angry dog might do.

During the various prayer battles, more than a score of unclean spirits came out of this woman, each identifying himself by name as he made his exit. This is a well-known phenomenon of dispossession, and not a fantastic oddity in the history of demon manifestations. Finally the woman was completely and joyfully delivered. All attempts of the spirits to regain possession were thwarted by steadfast prayer and resistance, as the woman's tongue was loosed to confess and praise the name of Jesus Christ as Savior and Deliverer.

The occultly oppressed must confess their sins of occult involvement. Victims of occult domination must first trust Christ and confess him as Savior from the penalty of sin and Deliverer from the powers of darkness. This remains the starting point in liberation from evil spirits. The reason is simple. One is not saved by confessing occult sins. To be saved, man must first recognize that he is a lost sinner, guilty of having broken the moral law of God and unable to please God. Only by trusting Christ as Redeemer can he find acceptance before a just and holy God. Thus man is reconciled to God through Jesus Christ who can save him and keep him from evil.

Therefore, the victim must first be saved, and then deal with the problem of occult deliverance. The occult involvement and transgression must then be confessed to a merciful God who will not abandon his children to the wicked one.

In the case of the Christian woman just cited, who had come under extreme demon domination to the point of possession, several years passed before she sought deliverance and made a full confession of her actions. But even then there was still no proper realization of sin, but merely a desire to be free from the spirit-control exercised over her life. Only when the woman through the help of prayer by others fully recognized and renounced the sin of complicity with the works of darkness was she delivered.[17]

By confessing the specific sins of occult involvement, a victim unmasks the enemy and exposes the stratagems by which he is held in bondage. If the sin is not disclosed, or if confession of it is refused after it is disclosed, Satan remains concealed, protected behind the unrecognized or unconfessed sin, free to continue his work of oppression and confusion.

In all cases, pastor-counselors should study the case history of the victim and try to establish if there were previous instances of occult involvement in the family. Only as these are ferreted out, their sinfulness recognized and confessed (Exodus 20:3-5), can deliverance come to the oppressed. Occult participation is a violation of the first commandment prohibiting idolatry. It dishonors God, and the punishment runs through the line of God-hating idolaters (Exodus 20:5), a principle Satan knows well and uses to his advantage.

All occult participation must be confessed, if deliverance is to be obtained. The victim should single out each specific form of occult involvement and confess it to God as a heinous sin. Confessions should run somewhat as follows: "Heavenly Father, I confess that I have sinned against you and your Word by following the horoscope, by seeking physical healing on some principle not sanctified by your Word, or through some sect unsound in doctrine, by consulting a fortune-teller, by attending a séance or a 'spiritualistic' meeting, by using an Ouija board or Tarot cards, or by having warts removed by magical charming, etc. I recognize these practices as grievous sins, and I renounce them completely in Jesus' name."

Because these sins opened the life to the powers of darkness, confessing and renouncing them not only uncovers the enemy's presence but furnishes him clear direction for exit, and bars the door against his further intrusion once he has gone.[18]

The occultly oppressed must renounce the Devil and command him to depart. This is essential when a pact has been concluded with the powers of darkness. Such a pact must be invalidated and annulled and can only be dissolved by a conscious act of repudiation on the part the one subjected, since Christ has already furnished the ground for this dissolution (Colossians 1:13). Says Dr. O. Riecker, "Everywhere where magical-occult or enchanting activities are practiced, an official confession may be necessary, a confession of liberation from all demonic powers, a repudiation of the devil in the words, 'I repudiate the devil and all his works.' "[19]

The renunciation must be a direct command to Satan himself (not a prayer or a request) to depart in Jesus' name. Satan's contention in the case of occult participation is that he has the right to enter when a person opens the door for him. He refuses to leave until that very person commands him to depart. This is why severely occult-oppressed people need help in prayer. They need aid to resist Satan and to exert their own will, strengthened by the Holy Spirit, to overcome the satanic will. If a patient fails to do this and depends solely upon the prayers of others, he will not experience complete or permanent emancipation.

This renunciation of Satan can be compared to the repudiation of paganism by converts in the early Church who renounced the demonic idol-cult (cf. 1 Corinthians 10:19, 20). Renunciation of the Devil by the victim of occult enslavement involves liberation from the demon-cult, for magic is a cult of the Devil and demons. The Greek word for renunciation basically means: "stepping out of the line of battle." He who repudiates the Devil steps out of his line of battle and becomes a soldier in the army of Jesus Christ in the fight against evil powers.

The occultly oppressed person experiences liberation through the greatness of God's power. If the demonic oppression is light, the victim can be liberated by accepting Christ, confessing occult involvement, and ordering Satan to depart without any outside help. But if the enslavement by evil powers is severe, outside help is required. In such instances, the sufferer under attack is unable to confess sin or to trust Christ on his own. Others must fight the battle for him until he receives strength and freedom to cooperate and claim deliverance.

Dick Hillis of Overseas Crusades narrates the case of a demon-possessed woman who was delivered while he and his wife were serving the Lord in the province of Honan, China. The husband of the victim, a young soldier, knocked at the missionaries' door one day, begging them to help his wife who suffered from suicidal mania. Twice the young husband had rescued her — once from hanging and on another occasion from drowning. Since the soldier was being called back to his battalion, he was at his wits' end what to do about his wife. So he brought her to the missionaries with the words, "I have heard that Christ is able to heal those who are demon-possessed, so I have brought her to you."

The missionaries took the woman and began to pray for her deliverance. But as they prayed, the demon-possessed victim would use the words from their prayer to compose ridiculous poems, at the same time screaming and making fun of what they were doing. For three days the prayer struggle continued, to no avail. On the third day, when the soldier came to get his wife, the missionaries asked for more time, and ordered the young husband to go home and destroy every vestige of idolatry.

The next morning the missionaries found the woman weeping uncontrollably, declaring that her home had been destroyed. This was actually the evil spirit speaking out of its victim's body and using her vocal cords to acknowledge that the soldier had indeed destroyed the idols. When the husband returned, he confirmed the fact.

At this juncture, as the missionaries were reading the Epistle to the Ephesians, the Holy Spirit suddenly made it transparently clear that they were not only identified with Christ in his death and his resurrection, but that they were "seated with Christ in heavenly places far above principalities and powers" (Ephesians 1:20-23), identified as well with him in his ascension in the heavenly places. Taking this new position of authority in Christ,[20] the missionaries and a Christian postmaster sang in the presence of the woman, "There's power in the blood," and after singing, they commanded the demon to come out of the woman in the name of Jesus. She was instantly delivered![21]

An instance of this sort shows that liberation from occult domination can come only through the greatness of God's power to us who believe (Ephesians 1:19). The conflict is not to be grounded in ourselves, in our praying, singing, or anything we are or can do, but wholly in what Christ has done for us and what we are in him. In Christ we are crucified, dead, buried, risen, ascended on high, and united with him in heavenly places, far above the realm of evil. It is not enough to pray and sing, though Satan hates both prayer and song. We must resist the Devil and command him to depart on the basis of God's authority and power who on Calvary "delivered us from the power of darkness" and "translated us into the kingdom of his dear Son" (Colossians 1:13). Christ's victorious conflict with the evil one (Ephesians 6:10-20) is the basis of deliverance from occult oppression and enslavement, as well as the ground of all progress in the Christian life.

In the case of the woman described earlier who became infested with over a score of evil spirits as the result of complicity with spiritualism, the final liberation from the dark powers was not accomplished without the most intense and unremitting battle in which Christ's victory was claimed. Each of the many demons that were expelled identified himself by name as he left the body of the victim. The last demon to go was "an unclean spirit," like those so often mentioned in the Gospel accounts (Matthew 10:1; 12:43; Mark 1:23, 26; 5:2, etc.) who are associated with immorality and sexual uncleanness. He styled himself by the name of "Internal Masculinity Cacoethes," and remained lodged in the sexual part of the being, and seemed impossible to dispel until the praying believers pressed the authority of God's Word and the power of the victorious Christ. When this last remaining unclean spirit finally made his exit through the victim's mouth, the woman almost strangled to death. But immediately upon deliverance, she began to praise God with freedom and joyful gratitude, completely and permanently set free.[22]

The occultly liberated must realize that deliverance is a walk as well as an experience. After deliverance it is necessary to walk in the will of God according to the Word of God, meticulously avoiding any complicity with Satan and his works. The ground wrested from Satan must be safeguarded for Christ. Jesus warns that evil powers may return if the delivered one capitulates to Satan and opens the door once again to him (Matthew 12:43-45). Unless the life of the liberated soul is filled with faith, an evil spirit can return, bringing seven other spirits more wicked than himself, so that the last state is worse than the first.

Those emancipated from occult power must keep clear of any form of occult practice. Contact with spiritistically oriented religions or any type of false or unsound doctrine should be avoided. It is also imperative, without any consideration of cost or value, to destroy all occult literature and occult objects. Books on magic and literature promoting cults and spiritism must go (cf. Acts 19:18, 19). Fortune-telling cards, Ouija boards, occult games, horoscopes, fetishes, charms, and all similar objects are to be done away with once and for all.

That riddance of occult objects and literature is indispensable to sustain emancipation from demon power is illustrated by a case of demon expulsion which took place near the Southern Presbyterian Station of Kiangyin, Kiangsu, China. There Mr. and Mrs. Ying, peasant farmers, were blessed with the birth of a third son, but Mrs. Ying was cursed with demon possession. Their farmer neighbors did not view demon possession as a strange phenomenon. Chinese peasants see much of it, and recognize it for what it is. There are, however, no institutions to care for such afflicted people. For those who do not know Christ there is no hope in such cases, except the futile prayers of the Buddhist priests. The Yings had paid highly for these, but to no avail. They were exceedingly unhappy, despite their good fortune to have three sons.

Then one day good news came to the distraught family. In the chapel in Sah-Kah-Lee, there were Christians who could deliver from demons in the name of Jesus. Since all else had failed, Mr. Ying in desperation sent for the elders of this church. When the little band of Bible-believing Christians reached the house, Mrs. Ying was lying in a coma on the bed, completely rigid, as in death.

Mr. Ying invited the elders in, but they refused to enter the house until he agreed to destroy everything that had been used to worship the gods and spirits. This was a lot to expect from someone who had trusted in idols all his life, but his plight was so desperate that he consented. Soon the family gods, kitchen gods, the ancestral shrine, and even the bits of paper on the front door blessed by the Buddhist priests were all destroyed.

After this was accomplished, the Christians held a praise and prayer service in the living room. Then, in simple faith the elders entered the bedroom and in the name of Jesus commanded the demon to come out of the prostrate woman. Mrs. Ying emerged at once from the coma, sat up, and cried out, "There he is (meaning the demon) in the corner!" And then, "There he goes out of the window!"

Among the crowd that jammed and surrounded the house, was a man standing on a bench peering in through the small aperture that served as a window. He fell off the seat and died the next day, whether from the fleeing demon or fright, God only knows. One thing is sure; Mrs. Ying was completely delivered and experienced no more trouble. Her whole family turned to Christ. The three sons became evangelists instead of ancestor-worshipers.

An interesting sequel to the story, which stresses the need of destroying every vestige of occultism, took place a short time after Mrs. Ying was delivered. The Christians told the Yings that the tree in front of their house, which had been used as a shrine, had to be cut down. Although the Yings protested their fear of the demons, as did the elders themselves, knowing full well Satan's power in pagan lands, they nevertheless cut the tree down, without the least harm, since the power of the demon could not touch those who were new creatures in Christ, and who had made a clean break with idolatry.[23]

But the walk that should characterize those liberated from the power of darkness is not merely a negative course of separation from occult art and practice. It is primarily a positive affirmation of strong faith and new life in Christ so that the delivered person will indeed be strong in the Lord. This requires faithful study and obedience of the Word of God. Our Lord used God's Word to chase the tempter (Matthew 4:1-11) and we shall chase him by the same means (Revelation 12:11). Those whose minds and hearts are filled with love for Christ and the Word of God are a terror to Satan.

A person liberated from occult power should also develop a

consistent prayer life. Prayer maintains vital contact with God, where Satan's attacks become powerless (Luke 18:1; Ephesians 6:18; 1 Thessalonians 5:17; Jude 20). It is important also to maintain communion with God through Christ as well as fellowship with other believers. One who has suffered demonic enslavement especially needs the awareness of God's presence and the company of other Christians for mutual encouragement and edification (1 John 1:3—2:2; Acts 2:41-47; Hebrews 10:24, 25).

The liberated person should also be a faithful witness, not only by word of mouth but by consistency of life. This is how he wages a successful campaign of resistance against Satan and his demon aides. After liberation Satan may seek to bring his former victims under his sway again. Through temptation the evil one will do all in his power to gain access to the life of a liberated individual.[24] As Barnhouse observes: "There is no armistice in this invisible war. What may appear to be only a skirmish may in reality be a major engagement. The importance of a spiritual battle is not to be measured by the number of troops engaged but by the principles involved, and above all by the exhibition of another phase of the impotence of any will that is not the will of God."[25]

In the hundreds of millions of battles fought every day in the invisible spiritual war, "the field of each battle is the heart of man."[26] And the man who has once known Satan's oppression must especially not "give place to the devil" (Ephesians 4:27) but "resist" him, that the evil one might flee from him (James 4:7). The believer must always rejoice in his union with his resurrected, ascended Lord in the heavenlies "far above all principalities and power" (Ephesians 1:20-23), where he stands in a position of triumph over sin and the powers of darkness.

As the believer counts upon and enjoys the power of his position in the Lord (Romans 6:11), life will become a vibrant experience of the all-conquering Christ manifesting himself in majestic victory and glory. The Christian's testimony, liberated from all the powers of evil, becomes that of the intrepid apostle: "I am crucified with Christ: nevertheless, I live;

yet not I, but Christ liveth in me; and the life which I now live in the flesh I live by the faith of the Son of God, who loved me and gave himself for me" (Galatians 2:20).

NOTES
CHAPTER 9

1. Cf. Hobart E. Freeman, *Deliverance from Occult Oppression and Subjection*, pp. 3-11.
2. *Life*, 68, no. 1 (January 9, 1970): 23.
3. *Ibid.*
4. Cf. T. J. Altizer and W. Hamilton, *Radical Theology and the Death of God.* Cf. Billy Graham, "God Is Not Dead," *U. S. News and World Report* (April 25, 1966), pp. 74-82.
5. This is the inescapable interpretation of this passage suggested by the context. The Holy Spirit who came in a distinctive sense to form and indwell the Church at Pentecost (John 14:16-20) will leave in that distinctive sense when the Church is completed.
6. Cf. Donald Grey Barnhouse, *The Invisible War,* pp. 270-277; Lewis Sperry Chafer, *Satan,* pp. 1-172; Chafer, *Systematic Theology,* 2 (1947): 28-121; John F. Walvoord, *Jesus Christ Our Lord,* pp. 258-290; J. Dwight Pentecost, *Things to Come,* pp. 412-424.
7. W. E. Vine, *An Expository Dictionary of New Testament Words,* 17th printing, 4:52. Concerning Revelation 9:20, 21, Walter Scott observes: "These two closing verses of the chapter reveal an astonishing picture of human depravity" (*Exposition of the Revelation of Jesus Christ,* p. 214).
8. Cf. Hobart E. Freeman, *Angels of Light?*, pp. 47-55. Cf. Edward M. Bounds, *Satan: His Personality, Power and Overthrow,* pp. 111-157; C. S. Lovett, *Dealing with the Devil,* pp. 77-112; Charles H. Usher, *Satan, A Defeated Foe,* pp. 5-69.
9. Kurt E. Koch, *Christian Counseling and Occultism,* pp. 28-153, and *Between Christ and Satan,* pp. 200-254.
10. Koch, *Christian Counseling,* p. 52.
11. For the question, Can a believer actually become demon-possessed?, see chapter 6, "Demons and Demon Possession."
12. See *Life*, 18, no. 1 (January 1970): 20-24.
13. Quoted in *Christian Heritage,* 31, no. 2 (February 1970): 19.
14. Gerhard Kloos M.D., *Grundriss der Psychiatrie und Neurologie* (Munich: Verlag-Müller and Steinicke, 1951), p. 424.
15. Koch, *Christian Counseling,* pp. 262-264.
16. J. A. MacMillan, *Modern Demon Possession,* pp. 3-5.
17. *Ibid.,* pp. 3, 5.
18. For the danger to the Christian of psychoanalysis at the hands of non-Christian psychotherapists and as a substitute for confession, see Koch, *Christian Counseling,* pp. 264, 265; cf. also the German neurologist, Dr. Enke, "Psychotherapy and Confession" in *Der Weg zur Seele* (Göttingen: Thomas, Vanderhoek, and Ruprecht, eds.), pp. 49-51f.

19. O. Riecker, *Die seelesorgerliche Begegnung* (Gütersloh, Bertelsmann Verlag, 1948), p. 81.
20. For this authoritative concept of prayer as standing upon one's position of unity with Christ, see J. A. MacMillan, *The Authority of the Intercessor,* pp. 3-20.
21. Dick Hillis, "Prayer was not enough: China," *Demon Experiences in Many Lands,* pp. 37-40.
22. MacMillan, pp. 4, 5.
23. Jean Bryans Lowen, "Blessed But Demon-Possessed," *Demon Experiences in Many Lands,* pp. 96-98.
24. Barnhouse, pp. 137-154.
25. Barnhouse, p. 137.
26. Barnhouse, *loc. cit.*

Bibliography

Adams, Evangeline. *Astrology for Everyone*. New York: Dodd, Mead and Co., 1931.

Ahmed, Rollo. *The Black Art*. London: Arrow Books, Ltd., 1966.

Albright, W. F. *From the Stone Age to Christianity*. Baltimore: Johns Hopkins Press, 1940.

Alexander, William M. *Demonic Possession in the New Testament*. Edinburgh: T. and T. Clark, 1902.

Altizer, T. J. and Hamilton, W. *Radical Theology and the Death of God*. New York: The Bobbs-Merrill Co., Inc., 1966.

Barnhouse, Donald Grey. *The Invisible War*. Grand Rapids: Zondervan Publishing House, 1965.

Bauer, Paul. *Wizards That Peep and Mutter*. Westwood, N. J.: Fleming H. Revell Co., 1967.

Bender, Hans. *Psychische Automatismen*. Leipzig: Freiburg, Verlag-Barth, 1936.

————————. *Zum Problem der ausserinnlichen Wahrnehmung*. Leipzig: Verlag-Barth, 1936.

Blonsdon, N. *A Popular Dictionary of Spiritualism*. New York: Fernhill House, Ltd., 1962.

Bounds, Edward M. *Satan: His Personality, Power, and Overthrow*. Grand Rapids: Baker Book House, 1963.

Braden, Charles S. *Christian Science Today*. Dallas, Tex.: Southern Methodist University Press, 1958.

Canaan, Taufik. *Demonenglaube im Lande der Bibel*. Leipzig: J. C. Hinrische Buchhandlung, 1929.

Castiglioni, Arturo. *Adventures of the Mind*. New York: Random House, 1947.

Chafer, Lewis Sperry. *Satan*. Chicago: Moody Press, 1942.

————————. *Systematic Theology*, II. Dallas, Tex.: Dallas Seminary Press, 1947.

Cicero, Marcus Tullius. *De Diviatione*. Ed. A. S. Pease. Urbana: University of Illinois, 1920.

Clark, Elmer T. *The Small Sects of America*. Rev. ed. New York: Abingdon-Cokesbury, 1949.

Daraul, Arkon. *Witches and Sorcerers*. London: Tandem Books, Ltd., 1965.

Davies, T. Witton. *Magic, Divination, and Demonology Among the Hebrews and Their Neighbors*. London: James Clark and Co., 1898.

Delaporte, Father. *The Devil: Does He Exist? And What Does He Do?* New York: D. and J. Sadlier and Co., 1871.

Demon Experiences in Many Lands. Chicago: Moody Press, 1960.

Diepgen, Paul. *Medizin und Kultur.* Stuttgart: Ferdinand Enke-Verlag, 1938.

Dixon, Jeane. *My Life and Prophecies.* New York: William Morrow and Co., 1969.

Doyle, A. Conan. *The History of Spiritualism.* 2 vols. New York: Doubleday, Doran & Co., 1926.

Edersheim, Alfred. *The Life and Times of Jesus the Messiah.* New York: Longmans, Green and Co., 1940.

Ellis, A. J. *The Divining Rod, A History of Water Witching.* Washington, D. C.: U. S. Geological Survey, 1917.

Encyclopedia Americana.

Encyclopaedia Brittanica.

Fell, John. *Demoniacs.* London: Charles Dilly, 1779.

Frazer, James George. *The Golden Bough: A Study in Magic and Religion.* New York: Macmillan Co., 1935.

Freeman, Hobart. *Angels of Light?* Plainfield, N. J.: Logos International, 1969.

.... *Deliverance from Occult Oppression and Subjection.* Claypool, Ind.: Faith Publications, 1968.

Gaebelein, A. C. *The Annotated Bible,* Vol. 4. New York: *Our Hope* Publication Office, 1913-1921.

Gardner, Gerald B. *Witchcraft Today.* London: Arrow Books, Ltd., 1965.

Gasson, Raphael. *The Challenging Counterfeit.* Plainfield, N. J.: Logos International, 1966.

Gibb, H. A. R. *Modern Trends in Islam.* Chicago: Cambridge, 1947.

Goldston, Robert. *Satan's Disciples.* New York: Ballantine Books, 1962.

Gray, James M. *Spiritism and the Fallen Angels.* Westwood, N. J.: Fleming H. Revell Co., 1920.

Hanson, E. F. *Demonology or Spiritualism, Ancient and Modern.* Belfast, Maine: published by the author, 1884.

Hesiod. *Works and Days.* Translated by Richard Lattimore. Ann Arbor, Mich.: University of Michigan Press, 1959.

Hodge, A. A. *Outlines of Theology.* New York: A. C. Armstrong and Son, 1891.

Hodge, Charles. *Systematic Theology II,* reprint. Grand Rapids, Mich.: W. B. Eerdmans, n.d.

Holtom, D. C. *Modern Japan and Shinto Nationalism,* revised ed. New York: Paragon Book Reprint Corp., 1947.

.... *The National Faith of Japan.* New York: Paragon Book Reprint Corp., 1938.

Holzer, Hans. *The Psychic World of Bishop Pike.* New York: Crown Publishers, 1970.

International Standard Bible Encyclopedia. Grand Rapids: W. B. Eerdmans, 1939.

The Interpreter's Dictionary of the Bible. New York: Abingdon Press, 1962.

Irvine, William C. *Heresies Exposed,* 11th ed. New York: Loizeaux Bros., 1940.

Jamieson, Fausset, Brown Commentary. Grand Rapids: W. B. Eerdmans, 1967.

Jastrow, Morris. *Hebrew and Babylonian Traditions.* New York: Scribner's Sons, 1911.

Josephus, Flavius. *Life and Works of Josephus.* Philadelphia: Winston Co., n.d.

Jung-Stilling. *Theorie der Geisterkunde.* Nurnberg: Zeitbuchverlag, 1921.

Kallas, James. *Jesus and the Power of Satan.* Philadelphia: Westminster Press, 1968.

Kloos, Gerhard. *Grundriss der Psychiatrie und Neurologie.* Munich: Verlag-Müller and Steinicke, 1951.

Köberle, A. *Die Seele des Christentums.* Berlin: Furch-Verlag, 1932.

Koch, Kurt E. *Between Christ and Satan.* Grand Rapids: Kregel Publications, 1961.

——————. *Christian Counseling and Occultism.* Translated by Andrew Petter. Grand Rapids: Kregel Publications, 1965.

Langton, G. Edward. *Essentials of Demonology.* London: The Epworth Press, 1949.

Larsen, Martensen. *Das Blendwerk des Spiritismus und die Rätsel der Seele.* Agentur des Rauhen Hauses, 1924.

Lindsay, Gordon. *Jeane Dixon — Prophetess or Psychic Medium?* San Antonio, Tex.: Christian Jew Publications, n.d.

Lovett, C. S. *Dealing with the Devil.* Baldwin Park, Calif.: Personal Christianity, 1967.

MacKenzie, Kenneth. *Our Physical Heritage in Christ.* Westwood, N. J.: Fleming H. Revell Co., 1923.

MacMillan, J. A. *The Authority of the Intercessor.* Harrisburg, Pa.: Christian Publications, Inc., 1942.

——————. *Modern Demon Possession.* Harrisburg, Pa.: Christian Publications, Inc., n.d.

McCrossan, T. J. *Bodily Healing and the Atonement.* Seattle, Wash.: T. J. McCrossan Publisher, 1930.

M'Donald, W. *Spiritualism Identical with Ancient Sorcery, New Testament Demonology, and Modern Witchcraft.* New York: Carlton and Porter, 1866.

Michelet, Jules. *Satanism and Witchcraft.* New York: Citadel Press, 1946.

Montgomery, Ruth. *A Gift of Prophecy.* New York: Morrow, William and Co., 1965.

Nevius, John L. *Demon Possession and Allied Themes,* 5th ed. Westwood, N. J.: Fleming H. Revell Co., n.d.

Newman, Albert Henry. *A Manual of Church History.* Philadelphia: American Baptist Publication Society, 1919.

New Schaff-Herzog Encyclopedia of Religious Knowledge. Grand Rapids: Baker Book House, n.d.

Oesterreich, T. K. *Possession, Demonical and Other Among Primitive Races in Antiquity, the Middle Ages, and Modern Times.* New York: R. Long and R. Smith, Inc., 1930.

Payne, P. D. and Bendit, L. J. *Psychic Sense.* Wheaton, Ill.: Theosophical Publishing House, 1961.

Pember, G. H. *Earth's Earliest Ages and Their Connection with Modern Spiritualism and Theosophy,* revised and enlarged edition of *Earth's Earliest Ages and Their Lessons for Us,* 1876. Westwood, N. J.: Fleming H. Revell Co., *ca.* 1900.

Penn-Lewis, Mrs. and Roberts, Evan. *War on the Saints.* London: Marshall Brothers, 1912.

Pentecost, J. Dwight. *Things to Come.* Findley, Ohio; Dunham Publishing Co., 1958.

Pike, Diane Kennedy. *Search.* New York: Doubleday and Co., 1970.

Pike, James A. and Kennedy, Diane. *The Other Side.* New York: Dell Publishing Co., 1969.

Pitt, Malcolm. *Introducing Hinduism.* New York: Friendship Press, 1955.

Porter, K. H. *Through a Glass Darkly.* New York: Grossman Publishers, Inc., 1958.

Pritchard, J. B. *Ancient Near Eastern Texts.* Princeton, N. J.: Princeton University, rev. ed., 1955.

Rhine, J. B. et al. *Extra-Sensory Perception after Sixty Years.* Boston: Crescendo Publishers, 1967.

——————and Pratt, J. G. *Parapsychology.* Springfield, Ill.: C. C. Thomas, 1958 ed.

Riecker, O. *Die seelesorgerliche Begegnung.* Gütersloh: Bertelsmann Verlag, 1948.

Rogers, R. W. *The Religion of Babylonia and Assyria.* New York: Eaton and Mains, 1908.

Schäble, Walter. *Der grosse Zauber.* Gladbeck: Schriften-missionsverlag, 1950.

Scott, Walter. *The Existence of Evil Spirits Proved.* London: Jackson and Walford, 1853.

——————. *Exposition of the Revelation of Jesus Christ,* 4th ed. London: Pickering and Inglis, n.d.

Schrenck-Notzing, Baron. *Matérialisationphänomene.* Munich: Reinhardt, 1914.

Schwendimann, Hans. *Wahrsagerei und ihre Folgen.* St. Gallen: Kommissionsverlag, Evangelische Buchhandlung, n.d.

Seligman, Kurt. *The History of Magic.* New York: Pantheon Books, Inc., 1948.

Simpson, A. B. *The Gospel of Healing.* New York: The Christian Alliance Publishing, revised ed. 1955.

Seabrook, William. *Witchcraft.* New York: Harcourt Brace & Co., 1940.

Smith, Susy. *The Enigma of Out-of-Body Travel.* New York: The New American Library, 1968.

Sommers, Montague. *The History of Witchcraft.* New Hyde Park, N.Y.: University Books, 1956.

Steiger, Brad. *Sex and Satanism.* New York: Ace Publishing Co., 1969.

Strong, Augustus. *Systematic Theology.* Philadelphia: The Judson Press, 1907.

Terhune, Albert Payson and Terhune, Anice. *Across the Line.* New York: Dutton and Co., 1945.

Thompson, R. Campbell. *Semitic Magic.* London: Luzac and Co., 1908.

Thorndike, Lynn. *A History of Magic and Experimental Science.* New York: Macmillan Co. and Columbia University Press, 1923-1941.

Torrey, C. C. *The Jewish Foundaton of Islam.* New York: Ktav Publishing House, Inc., 1933.

Townsend, L. T. *Satan and Demons.* Cincinnati: Jennings and Pye, 1902.

Tylor, E. B. *Primitive Culture.* New York: G. P. Putnam's Sons, Knickerbocker Press, 1924.

Unger, Merrill F. *The Baptizing Work of the Holy Spirit.* Grand Rapids: Zondervan Publishing House, 1964.

————————. *Biblical Demonology.* Wheaton, Ill.: Scripture Press, 1952.

————————. *Principles of Expository Preaching.* Grand Rapids: Zondervan Publishing House, 1955.

Usher, Charles H. *Satan, A Defeated Foe.* Fort Washington, Pa.: Christian Literature Crusade, n.d.

Van Baalen, Jan K. *The Chaos of the Cults,* 7th ed. Grand Rapids: W. B. Eerdmans, 1948.

Vine, W. E. *An Expository Dictionary of New Testament Words,* 17th printing. Westwood, N. J:. Fleming H. Revell Co., 1966.

Visser t'Hooft, W. A. *The Meaning of Ecumenical.* Petersborough, N. H.: Bauhan, William, Inc., 1954.

Wallace, C. H. *Witchcraft in the World Today.* New York: Board Books, 1967.

Walvoord, John F. *Jesus Christ Our Lord.* Chicago: Moody Press, 1969.

Wright, Elbee. *Book of Legendary Spells.* Minneapolis, Minn.: Marlor Publishing Co., 1968.